Blake, Clarence N.

QUIZ BOOK ON BLACK AMERICA

QUIZ BOOK

ON BLACK AMERICA

QUIZ BOOK ON BLACK AMERICA

**Clarence N. Blake, Ed.D.
and Donald F. Martin, Ph.D.**

**Decorations by
Rosalyn Hawthorne**

Houghton Mifflin Company Boston 1976

ACKNOWLEDGMENTS

Scores of sources have been invaluable in compiling a book of this nature. The authors are extremely grateful to the Afro-Am Publishing Company of Chicago for their permission to use a portion of *Great Negroes, Past and Present* by Dr. Russell L. Adams (who also wrote the Foreword); the Johnson Publishing Company, also of Chicago, for their permission to use a portion of the *Ebony Handbook*, edited by Doris E. Saunders; and to Dodd, Mead & Company, New York, for their permission to use sections of *Famous Black Entertainers of Today* by Raoul Abdul.

The authors are especially indebted to Mary K. Harmon and Perry Israel of Houghton Mifflin Company for their invaluable editorial assistance.

Library of Congress Cataloging in Publication Data

Blake, Clarence N
Quiz book on Black America.

SUMMARY: More than seventy quizzes challenge and increase the reader's knowledge of the roles played by blacks in American life.
1. Afro-Americans — Miscellanea — Juvenile literature. [1. Afro-Americans — Miscellanea. 2. Questions and answers] I. Martin, Donald F., joint author. II. Title.
E185.B6 973'.04'96073 76-22210
ISBN 0-395-24389-0
ISBN 0-395-24974-0 pbk.

Printed in the United States of America.
V 10 9 8 7 6 5 4 3 2 1

Dedicated to the memory
of Dr. Carter G. Woodson,
and his dream to
have black history documented.

CONTENTS

FOREWORD

As the academic aspects of the Black Studies revolution settled down toward becoming a rather definite area of intellectual concern, the need for teaching aids and instructional learning devices increased. During the last decade many works on every conceivable aspect of the Afro-American experience have been produced. General readers have often been confused by the welter of conflicting "facts" and assertions, even as better research approaches and techniques generate ever-more reliable data. As with most emerging fields of inquiry, the Black Studies movement is now approaching a period of regrouping and synthesis. One of the best aids for facilitating such a reorganization is a teaching and learning device that condenses hundreds of statements and assertions into a carefully designed set of questions. *Quiz Book on Black America* is a book that does this for a number of aspects of the black experience.

The book subdivides the black experience into approximately twenty areas, including civil rights, judicial decisions, movies, entertainment, sports, inventions, the labor movement, education, pioneers in business, literature, medicine, fraternal and social uplift associations, publishing, religion and the institution of slavery. Using *Quiz Book on Black America,* it is possible for readers to check their general knowledge, construct game quizzes of their own and reduce research time in seeking answers to specific questions. Students will find this book helpful. Drs. Blake and Martin have built the questions in their book upon a solid basis of evidence and learning that represents a historically and sociologically sound condensation of the works of hundreds of researchers and writers. In performing this task, they have placed all of us in their debt.

Russell L. Adams, Ph.D.
Howard University
Washington, D.C.

INTRODUCTION

Since the beginning of the civil rights movement of the early 1960s, much attention has been directed toward understanding the contributions made by blacks to American culture. While documentation already illustrates that blacks had made innumerable contributions to the American way of life long before the middle of the twentieth century, their contributions have not received just recognition. As a result, there is a proliferation of books, magazines and instructional materials designed to raise the level of consciousness and pride among black people. Stereotyped notions about black people are no longer tolerated by those armed with a new level of awareness about black culture.

Factual information has helped dispel many myths related to blacks. Those who believed that blacks were lazy often found themselves amazed at the energy expended and creativity demonstrated in inventing important devices and improved ways of serving mankind.

Once exposed to facts relating to the Afro-American population, past and present, it is believed that some changes in attitudes might occur among those who previously knew little about blacks. Unfortunately, the attitude of many school officials in the United States has not been conducive to the establishment of comprehensive curricula that include the contributions of blacks in all areas of academic study. It may be some time before this is accomplished, but few public school officials can afford not to pay close attention to the thirst for facts about blacks that is found in their student populations and among parents of students.

This book of quizzes is not designed to provide a critical analysis of blacks in America. Many social scientists have accomplished that task most successfully. It is designed to offer factual information to be used as you, the reader, see fit.

The authors hope that readers will be entertained as they attempt to answer the questions. We have tried to make the acquisition of knowledge a pleasurable learning experience.

Clarence N. Blake
Donald F. Martin
Washington, D.C.
July, 1976

QUIZ BOOK

ON BLACK AMERICA

Civil Rights

On February 1, 1960, four young men walked into the Woolworth's department store in uptown Greensboro, North Carolina, and sat at the lunch counter seeking service. They were directed to the "colored" section of the lunch counter. Their actions at this point ushered in the civil rights movement of the 1960s: they refused to leave the seats they had occupied.

There had been other civil rights movements in this country prior to 1960, but none had the impact and was as well organized as this one. Roy Wilkins, Whitney Young, James Farmer, Martin Luther King, Jr., and countless others had been working for the human rights of the black man in America for centuries.

Although the Thirteenth, Fourteenth and Fifteenth amendments had been passed for several decades, blacks were not receiving the full benefits of citizenship guaranteed by the Constitution of the United States. Therefore, organizations such as the Congress of Racial Equality, the Southern Christian Leadership Conference and the National Association for the Advancement of Colored People directed their efforts toward the attainment of access to public accommodations, the right to vote and equal protection under the law.

The issues have changed from time to time. Some of the basic goals of the civil rights movement were attained while others were not. But preserving the rights of America's citizens should be a continuous concern of paramount importance to all of us.

CIVIL RIGHTS QUIZ 1

1. How many blacks from the U.S. have been awarded the Nobel Peace Prize?

   a. one **b. two** **c. three** **d. four**

2. In 1966, he took over the leadership of the Student Nonviolent Coordinating Committee and announced his policy of "Black Power," a political and social movement calling for removal of whites from leadership and policy-making positions within the civil rights organization. His name is:

   a. H. Rap Brown **b. Harold Featherstone** **c. Harland Randolph** **d. Stokely Carmichael**

3. The black protest movement of the sixties is credited with sparking the current fight on American racism. In what city and on what date did the protest movement get its start?

   a. Forest City, Arkansas, February 1, 1960
   b. Memphis, Tennessee, August 12, 1960
   c. Greensboro, North Carolina, February 1, 1960
   d. Durham, North Carolina, August 12, 1960

4. What was the first large city to integrate its lunch counters?

   a. San Antonio, Texas, March 16, 1960
   b. Atlanta, Georgia, March 16, 1960
   c. Nashville, Tennessee, July 11, 1959
   d. Little Rock, Arkansas, July 11, 1959

5. The Student Nonviolent Coordinating Committee (SNCC) was organized on this university campus on April 15, 16 and 17 in 1960.

   a. Shaw University
   b. Lincoln University
   c. Kentucky State University
   d. Jackson State University

6. On December 21, 1956, this city desegregated its entire public transportation system.

   a. Jackson, Mississippi
   b. Tampa, Florida
   c. Montgomery, Alabama
   d. Little Rock, Arkansas

7. The famous bus boycott of 1955 began in this city.

   a. Montgomery, Alabama
   b. Memphis, Tennessee
   c. Houston, Texas
   d. Jacksonville, Florida

8. The phrase "Black Power" originated in 1966, during the James Meredith peace march in this state.

   a. South Carolina **c. Georgia**
   b. Maryland **d. Mississippi**

9. The civil rights leader who assumed the leadership of the Southern Christian Leadership Conference when Dr. Martin Luther King, Jr., was assassinated was:

   a. Bayard Rustin **c. Ralph Abernathy**
   b. Stokely Carmichael **d. Whitney Young, Jr.**

10. He organized the March on Washington of 1963 and the first "freedom ride" in 1957.

    a. H. Rap Brown **c. Lester B. Granger**
    b. Vernon Jordan **d. Bayard Rustin**

---

1. two. Dr. Ralph Bunche and Dr. Martin Luther King, Jr. 2. Stokley Carmichael 3. Greensboro, North Carolina, when four college students from North Carolina State University sat in at a Woolworth's lunch counter on February 1, 1960 4. San Antonio, Texas, March 16, 1960 5. Shaw University 6. Montgomery, Alabama 7. Montgomery, Alabama 8. Mississippi 9. Ralph Abernathy 10. Bayard Rustin

---

CIVIL RIGHTS QUIZ 2

1. The first Civil Rights Act since 1875 was passed by Congress on:

   a. August 29, 1955 **c. August 29, 1957**
   b. August 29, 1956 **d. August 29, 1960**

2. The Twenty-fourth Amendment, abolishing poll taxes, was passed in:

a. **1958** c. **1964**
b. **1960** d. **1968**

3. Black History Week was introduced by Dr. Carter G. Woodson and the Association for the Study of Negro Life and History in:

a. **1916** c. **1936**
b. **1926** d. **1946**

4. Recently "Black History Week" was changed to "Black History Month." It is the month of:

a. **January** c. **March**
b. **February** d. **April**

5. When did Dr. Martin Luther King, Jr., receive the Nobel Peace Prize?

a. **December 10, 1962** c. **December 10, 1964**
b. **December 10, 1963** d. **December 10, 1965**

6. When did the Interstate Commerce Commission ban segregation in buses, in waiting rooms and in travel coaches involved in interstate travel?

a. **November 25, 1954** c. **November 25, 1956**
b. **November 25, 1955** d. **November 25, 1959**

7. Malcolm X was assassinated on:

a. **February 21, 1963** c. **February 21, 1965**
b. **February 21, 1964** d. **February 21, 1966**

8. When and where was CORE's first sit-in demonstration?

   a. 1943, in a restaurant in Chicago
   b. 1952, in a restaurant in Detroit
   c. 1944, in a restaurant in Cleveland
   d. 1945, in a restaurant in Greensboro

9. What institution has played the most important role as a force for black unity?

   a. NAACP
   b. SCLC
   c. CORE
   d. The Church

10. When was Dr. Martin Luther King, Jr., assassinated?

    a. April 4, 1967
    b. April 4, 1966
    c. April 4, 1968
    d. April 4, 1969

---

1. August 29, 1957 2. 1964 3. 1926 4. February 5. December 10, 1964 6. November 25, 1954 7. February 21, 1965 8. In 1943, in a restaurant in the Loop in Chicago 9. The Church 10. April 4, 1968, in Memphis, Tennessee

---

Education

While there were a few blacks and a few whites who were interested in the education of blacks prior to the War Between the States, it was not until the war was nearing its conclusion that institutions of higher education for blacks began to spring up in the South and other parts of the country. Most of these schools were located in the South because that is where the larger percentage of blacks lived.

Prior to the mid-1860s, there were "free" blacks who had received some schooling, but few of them had actually obtained a higher education. Attempts had been made to establish school systems in the South but they met great resistance from the white communities. Alexander Hays, a former slave, made a serious effort to set up a school system for blacks in Washington, D.C., in the 1850s. In 1858, after the schools had been systematically burned, Hays and his colleagues were run out of town. Most blacks were not prepared for higher education because they could not obtain a primary or secondary education. However, there was a small number that was afforded the opportunity of a college education and they took advantage of it. The first to receive their degrees did so in 1826 from colleges north of the Mason-Dixon line.

A central question that might be asked is, why did so many institutions of higher education spring up at the close of the Civil War? One answer, if only partial, is that education was viewed as a panacea for all the ills that confronted the newly freed men. Education was seen as an excellent tool for acculturization. Noble whites from the North who were bent on giving salvation to the ex-slave had a great deal to do with the establishment of a northern initiative to found higher education institutions for blacks. Many northerners felt it their moral responsibility to offer financial assistance to blacks interested in setting up colleges for the education of their people.

There was some debate over what sort of education blacks should receive. Some people advocated a vocational education while others advocated a liberal arts education. The debate raged for quite a while, until the founding of the land-grant institutions in 1890 that emphasized "mechanical, technical and normal" education for blacks. The notion that blacks were inferior to whites served as the basis for the Second Morrell Act of 1890. Primarily, private schools were not affected. With the exception of Tuskegee Institute, most private colleges emphasized a liberal arts education.

The two schools of thought regarding the education of the black man are primarily the products of Booker T. Washington and W. E. B. Du Bois. They both made great contributions to the nation in the area of education.

EDUCATION QUIZ 1

Match the following with the correct paragraph. There are twelve possible answers but only ten paragraphs. Some answers may be used more than once.

Daniel Payne	**W. E. B. Du Bois**
Booker T. Washington	**Mary McLeod Bethune**
Charlotte E. Ray	**Mordecai W. Johnson**
Alain L. Locke	**Lincoln University**
Carter G. Woodson	**William M. Trotter**
Bowdoin College	**Virgil L. Jones**

1. She was a scholar, the first woman to graduate from the Howard University School of Law and the first American woman to graduate from any law school in America.

2. He was a scholar, philosopher, historian, educator, literary critic and the first black to receive a Rhodes Scholarship.

3. He was an outstanding historian. He has been credited with writing the first book on black history. He is most noted for founding Black History Week.

4. He was the founder of Tuskegee Institute in Alabama. He was an outstanding leader and educator. He was educated at Hampton Institute in Virginia and helped set up the National Negro Business League.

5. A former bishop of the African Methodist Episcopal Church, he was the first black college president in America. Preceding his position at Wilberforce University, he was an educator of southern slaves in South Carolina until the school was forced to close after the Nat Turner rebellion.

6. He was the first black president of Howard University.
7. It is the oldest college in the U.S. that had as its original purpose higher education for blacks.
8. She was an educator, social worker and founder of a famous college in Florida.
9. It was the first American college to grant a degree to a black American (1826).
10. He was the first black scholar to be awarded a doctoral degree by Harvard University.

---

1. Charlotte E. Ray 2. Alain L. Locke 3. Carter G. Woodson 4. Booker T. Washington 5. Daniel Payne 6. Mordecai W. Johnson 7. Lincoln University 8. Mary McLeod Bethune 9. Bowdoin College 10. W. E. B. Du Bois

---

EDUCATION QUIZ 2

1. What is the approximate monetary value of the combined physical plants of the thirty-four black public colleges?
   a. over 800 million dollars
   b. over 600 million dollars
   c. over 400 million dollars
   d. over 200 million dollars

2. Which state has the greatest number of black public colleges?
   a. North Carolina
   b. Alabama
   c. Texas
   d. Arkansas

3. How many predominantly black public colleges are land-grant institutions?

   a. 12 c. 15
   b. 14 d. 16

4. What is the main problem facing black colleges in the 1970s?

   a. low enrollment c. financial woes
   b. faculty retention d. graduate placement

5. What percent of black college students attend black colleges?

   a. 50 percent c. 40 percent
   b. 25 percent d. 30 percent

6. Approximately how many full-time equivalent students are enrolled in traditionally black public colleges?

   a. 90,000 c. 110,000
   b. 100,000 d. 120,000

7. Of the thirty-four black *public* colleges, which one has the largest enrollment (as of 1976)?

   a. Howard University
   b. Prairie View University
   c. Southern University
   d. the University of the District of Columbia

8. Approximately how many bachelor's degrees are awarded annually at black public colleges?

   a. about 14,000 c. about 22,000
   b. about 16,000 d. about 26,000

9. In 1865, three colleges were founded for the education of blacks. They were:

   a. **Howard, J. C. Smith and Allen**
   b. **Talladega, Tuskegee and Lincoln**
   c. **Lane, Shaw and Morehouse**
   d. **Shaw, Atlanta and Virginia Union**

10. The first honorary degree ever offered to a black in the U.S. was by Harvard University in 1896 to:

   a. **W. E. B. Du Bois**
   b. **Booker T. Washington**
   c. **Adolphus Woodward**
   d. **Wendell P. Russell**

---

1. over 600 million dollars 2. North Carolina 3. 16 4. financial woes 5. 25 percent 6. 110,000 7. Southern University 8. about 16,000 9. Shaw, Atlanta and Virginia Union 10. Booker T. Washington

---

EDUCATION QUIZ 3

1. True/False Booker T. Washington stressed education in the liberal arts and the humanities. W. E. B. Du Bois stressed vocational education.

2. True/False Females outnumber males by about 3 percent in black public colleges.

3. True/False A black man was president of Georgetown University in Washington, D.C., from 1873 to 1882.

4. True/False Atlanta, Georgia, which houses the Atlanta University complex, is the nation's center of black education. There are five colleges and universities within the complex.

5. True/False The anchor of black communities in most American cities (excluding the church) has been the black institutions of higher education.

6. True/False Langston University in Oklahoma is older than the state of Oklahoma.

7. True/False The Methodist Episcopal Church established Wilberforce University near Xenia, Ohio, in 1856.

8. True/False The first black elected to the Hall of Fame was an educator named Booker T. Washington.

9. True/False The oldest public black college in the nation is Cheney State College in Cheney, Pennsylvania.

10. True/False Of the historically black public colleges, three are less than fifty years old. They are Norfolk State, Texas Southern and Mississippi Valley State College.

---

1. False. The opposite is true 2. True 3. True. Patrick Francis Healey, brother of the first black Catholic priest, was Georgetown's first president 4. True 5. True 6. True. Langston University was founded in 1897. The state of Oklahoma was admitted to the Union ten years later 7. True 8. True 9. True. Cheney State began in 1837 10. True. Norfolk State was founded in 1935; Texas Southern in 1947; and Mississippi Valley State in 1950

Elections and Appointments

Politics might be defined as human behavior as it relates to public affairs. It is in the political arena that decisions are made that determine how American life will be staged. When one views the small percentage of blacks in public decision-making roles, it is little wonder that whites make more decisions on behalf of blacks than blacks do themselves. The cry of "no taxation without representation" was uttered by a black man who did not have the privilege of full citizenship in Massachusetts.

Today, as in the past, when a black person is elected to local, state or national office, it is more newsworthy than if the elected had not been black. Blacks now serve as mayors, judges, local, state and federal officials and as top executives in other non-elected positions. Theoretically, under the generally accepted terms of a democratic society, being elected to public office places one in a position of influence, through which decisions about the lives of blacks can be made.

ELECTIONS AND APPOINTMENTS QUIZ 1

1. He was the first black *federal* judge.

   a. Clarence Laster
   b. William H. Hastie
   c. Hobart Taylor, Jr.
   d. Spottswood Robinson

2. Who was the first black woman to be appointed a *federal* judge?

   a. Constance Baker Motley
   b. Jeraldine F. Martin
   c. Hannah Elizabeth Byrd
   d. Juanita Kidd Stout

3. Who was the first black woman judge in the U.S.?

   a. Jane Matilda Bolin
   b. Majorie McKenzie Lawson
   c. Edith Spurlock Sampson
   d. Geraldine Bledsoe Ford

4. Who was the first black man to become a *lifetime* federal judge?

   a. Ervin C. Mollison
   b. William H. Hastie
   c. George Davenport
   d. Robert E. Bennett

5. Who was the first black jurist to hold a federal judgeship west of the Mississippi River?

   a. **David W. Williams** c. **Wade G. McCree**
   b. **Robert Morris** d. **Leroy U. Dudley**

6. What do Jane M. Bolin and Hannah E. Byrd have in common?

   a. **They were the first black women judges appointed in the U.S.**
   b. **They are both judges in Chicago, Illinois**
   c. **They are both graduates of the Howard University School of Law**
   d. **They married brothers who are also lawyers**

7. Who was the first black woman judge appointed by President Kennedy?

   a. **Marjorie McKenzie Lawson**
   b. **Betty Delores Smith**
   c. **Maggie Lawrence Miller**
   d. **Jearline Briscoe Terrell**

8. The black lawyer who on June 25, 1972, became the permanent chairman of the credentials committee of the Democratic National Convention was:

   a. **Clifford A. Alexander**
   b. **Clyde Clarence Ferguson**
   c. **Patricia Roberts Harris**
   d. **Walter E. Washington**

9. The black security guard who called the police to the Washington, D.C., Watergate complex to arrest five men who were breaking into the office of the Democratic National Headquarters was:

a. **Frank Wills**
b. **Oscar Griffin**
c. **Will Grissett**
d. **Charles Asbury**

10. The first black man to testify in court against a white man was:

    a. **John Philip, in 1624 at Jamestown, Virginia**
    b. **Havard Jones, in 1624 at Providence, Rhode Island**
    c. **Jefferson Cooper, in 1624 at Jamestown, Virginia**
    d. **Richard Nelson, in 1624 at Providence, Rhode Island**

---

1. William H. Hastie. In 1944, he was also appointed governor of the Virgin Islands. He was dean of the Howard University Law School in 1939 2. Constance Baker Motley was appointed a federal judge on January 25, 1966. A graduate of Columbia University School of Law, she served as a legal assistant to the NAACP and has won many cases in the area of civil rights 3. Jane Matilda Bolin was appointed to the court of domestic relations by Mayor La Guardia of New York, in 1939 4. Ervin C. Mollison, appointed by President Truman to the U.S. Customs Court in 1945 5. Robert Morris of Boston was appointed by Governor George N. Briggs in 1952 6. They were the first black women judges appointed *in the U.S. 7. Marjorie McKenzie Lawson, to the District of Columbia Juvenile Court 8. Patricia Roberts Harris 9. Frank Wills, on June 17, 1972 10. John Philip*

ELECTIONS AND APPOINTMENTS QUIZ 2

Match the following with the correct paragraph. There are twelve possible answers but only ten paragraphs. Some answers may be used more than once.

William L. Dawson	**Arthur Mitchell**
Amos Milburn	**Robert Morris**
James DePreist	**Shirley Chisholm**
Otis Redding and	**Leroy R. Johnson**
John Conyers	**Joe Frazier**
Adam Clayton Powell, Jr.	**Barbara Jordan and**
Oscar De Priest	**Andrew Young**

1. He was the first black congressman to chair a major congressional committee (House Committee on Government Operations, which handles expenditures).
2. He was the first congressman to introduce legislation to desegregate the armed forces.
3. In 1944, he was the first black congressman elected from the eastern part of the U.S.
4. In 1928, he was the first black congressman elected from a northern state.
5. In 1934, he became the first black Democrat of the twentieth century to be elected to Congress.
6. She was the first black woman elected to Congress.
7. She was the first black female to become a serious candidate for President of the U.S.
8. He was Georgia's first black state legislator since Reconstruction.

9. He was the first black man to speak before the South Carolina legislature since Reconstruction.

10. They were the first two blacks from the South to be elected to the House of Representatives since the turn of the century.

---

1. William L. Dawson of Chicago 2. Adam Clayton Powell, Jr., of New York 3. Adam Clayton Powell, Jr., of New York 4. Oscar De Priest of Illinois 5. Arthur Mitchell of Chicago 6. Shirley Chisholm of New York 7. Shirley Chisholm of New York 8. Leroy R. Johnson 9. Joe Frazier, a native of South Carolina 10. Barbara Jordan and Andrew Young

---

ELECTIONS AND APPOINTMENTS QUIZ 3

Match the following with the correct paragraph. There are twelve possible answers but only ten paragraphs. Some answers may be used more than once.

Dr. Melvin H. Evans	**Carl Stokes**
Dr. Therman Evans	**Walter E. Washington**
F. Q. Morton	**Frederick Douglass**
Samuel Lowery	**Joseph Jenkins Roberts**
Massachusetts	**Edward W. Brooke**
Michigan	**William L. Dawson**

1. He was the first *elected* governor of the Virgin Islands.

2. He was the first black commissioner in New York City.

3. It was the first northern state to elect blacks to its legislature.

4. He was the first black man to be elected attorney general in the U.S. (state of Massachusetts).
5. He is the first black U.S. senator since Reconstruction.
6. He was the first black admitted to the Supreme Court of Tennessee.
7. He was the first black marshal of the District of Columbia.
8. He was the first president of Liberia.
9. He was the first black man to head the government of a major American city (appointed).
10. He was the first black mayor of a major American city (1968).

---

1. Dr. Melvin H. Evans *was administered the oath by* Thurgood Marshall *on January 4, 1971* 2. Attorney F. Q. Morton 3. Massachusetts 4. Edward W. Brooke 5. Edward W. Brooke 6. Samuel Lowery *of Nashville. He was admitted to practice before the Supreme Court in 1880* 7. Frederick Douglass. *Luke Moore became the second black U.S. marshal of the District of Columbia on May 9, 1962* 8. Joseph Jenkins Roberts *(1809–1876), born of free parents in Petersburg, Va. He became president of Liberia in 1842* 9. Walter E. Washington *was appointed commissioner-mayor of Washington, D.C., by President Lyndon B. Johnson on November 7, 1967* 10. Carl Stokes *(Cleveland, Ohio)*

ELECTIONS AND APPOINTMENTS QUIZ 4

Match the following with the correct paragraph. There are twelve possible answers but only ten paragraphs. Some answers may be used more than once.

A. Dwight Petitt
Nollie G. Stowers
Maynard Jackson
Patricia R. Harris
Kenneth A. Gibson
Charles C. Diggs, Jr.
Barbara C. Jordan
John Conyers, Jr.
Charles H. Houston
Channing E. Phillips
Walter E. Washington
Edith Spurlock Sampson

1. He was the first black American to be elected mayor of a major *northeastern* city in the U.S.
2. He is chairman of the House Committee on the District of Columbia and the House Foreign Affairs Sub-committee on Africa.
3. She is the first black elected to Congress from the South in the twentieth century.
4. He was the first black member of the House Judiciary Committee, a unit with jurisdiction over civil rights legislation.
5. He (1895–1950) was considered one of the greatest constitutional lawyers of all times.
6. He was the first black man ever considered for nomination for president by a major national party. He was nominated at the Democratic convention in Chicago on August 28, 1968.
7. She was the first black delegate to the United Nations.
8. He is the first *elected* mayor of Washington, D.C.
9. She was the first black female ambassador in U.S. history.
10. He was the first black vice mayor and mayor in Atlanta, Georgia's history.

1. Kenneth A. Gibson became mayor of Newark, New Jersey, on June 16, 1970 2. Charles C. Diggs, Jr. 3. Barbara C. Jordan, Texas, 18th District, Democrat 4. John Conyers, Jr., Michigan, 1st District, Democrat 5. Charles H. Houston 6. Reverend Channing E. Phillips 7. Edith Spurlock Sampson was appointed on August 24, 1950 8. Walter E. Washington 9. Patricia R. Harris (Mrs. William B. Harris) was sworn in as ambassador to Luxembourg on July 6, 1965 10. Maynard Jackson

ELECTIONS AND APPOINTMENTS QUIZ 5

Match the following with the correct paragraph. There are twelve possible answers but only ten paragraphs. Some answers may be used more than once.

Thomas Johns	**Hobart Taylor, Jr.**
J. Ernest Wilkins	**William H. Lewis**
Carl T. Rowan	**Frank Reeves**
William H. Johnson	**Archibald J. Carey**
Leon Higginbottham	**Andrew F. Brimmer**
Arthur Mitchell	**E. Fredric Morrow**

1. He was the first black American appointed to assistant secretary level in the cabinet (Labor, May 4, 1954).
2. He was the first black member of the Federal Trade Commission.
3. He was the first black ever to address a Democratic National Convention.
4. He was the first black special assistant to President Kennedy.

5. He was the first black chairman of President Eisenhower's Committee on Employment Policy and a U.N. delegate.

6. He was the first black special assistant to President Eisenhower.

7. He was the first black assistant U.S. attorney general.

8. He was the first black appointed a governor on the Federal Reserve Board.

9. He was the first black member of the Export-Import Bank.

10. He was the first black person to sit on the National Security Council.

---

1. J. Ernest Wilkins 2. Arthur Mitchell 3. Leon Higginbotham 4. Frank Reeves 5. Archibald J. Carey 6. E. Frederic Morrow 7. William H. Lewis 8. Andrew F. Brimmer 9. Hobart Taylor, Jr. 10. Carl T. Rowan

---

Entertainment

In the spring of 1974, one of America's greatest entertainers died in New York City. Music was his mistress and he loved her madly. Edward Kennedy ("Duke") Ellington loved more than his music; he loved playing it for audiences all over the world. The pleasures derived from hearing "The Duke" play prompted many to bestow upon him numerous medals and awards, among them the presidential Medal of Freedom for his contributions to the music world.

The entertainment field stands out as an area in which countless blacks have gained national prominence. While other careers were limited and restrictive to blacks in the 1920s, '30s and '40s, good black entertainers could often play some of the "best houses" where their brothers and sisters could not enter.

Thanks to a large number of black entertainers, America

has been afforded the opportunity to get a glimpse of black culture in a positive light reflective of a great heritage in all areas of the entertainment industry.

ENTERTAINMENT QUIZ 1

What is (or was) the *specialty* of these performers?

Names	Scrambled Clues
1. Jelly Roll Morton	Singer
2. Bessie Smith	Pianist
3. Billie Holiday	Blues Singer
4. Duke Ellington	Blues Singer
5. Count Basie	Pianist/Composer
6. Lena Horne	Pianist
7. Ella Fitzgerald	Singer
8. Lionel Hampton	Drummer/Vibraharpist
9. Ray Charles	Singer/Pianist
10. Miles Davis	Trumpeter

---

1. Pianist 2. Blues Singer 3. Blues Singer 4. Pianist/Composer 5. Pianist 6. Singer 7. Singer 8. Drummer/Vibraharpist 9. Singer/Pianist 10. Trumpeter

---

ENTERTAINMENT QUIZ 2

What is (or was) the *specialty* of these performers?

Names	Scrambled Clues
1. Dizzy Gillespie	Trumpeter
2. Charlie Parker	Singer
3. Mahalia Jackson	Saxophonist
4. Clara Ward	Guitarist
5. Isaac Hayes	Gospel Singer
6. Huddie Ledbetter	Gospel Singer
7. Kenny Burrell	Singer/Composer
8. Dorothy Ashby	Harpist
9. Donald Byrd	Blues Singer/Guitarist
10. Johnny Mathis	Trumpeter

---

1. Trumpeter 2. Saxophonist 3. Gospel Singer 4. Gospel Singer 5. Singer/Composer 6. Blues Singer/Guitarist 7. Guitarist 8. Harpist 9. Trumpeter 10. Singer

---

ENTERTAINMENT QUIZ 3

1. Who was the first black man to devote his entire career to symphonic conducting?

   a. Dean Dixon | **c. Robert Noland**
   b. James DePreist | **d. Clarence Haynes**

2. Who was the first black to break the color bar in concert halls for black classical singers?

   a. Paul Robeson | **c. Lloyd Price**
   b. Roland Hayes | **d. Joe Tex**

3. What is the name of the first symphony that included black folksongs?

    a. **Brahm's First Symphony in 1884**
    b. **Chadwick's Second Symphony in 1886**
    c. **Franck's Second Symphony in 1886**
    d. **Dittersdorf's First Symphony in 1901**

4. When and where was the first all-black classical ballet company founded in the U.S.?

    a. **the Dance Theater of Philadelphia on June 6, 1971**
    b. **the Dance Theater of Harlem on January 6, 1971**
    c. **the Dance Theater of Chicago on January 6, 1971**
    d. **the Dance Theater of Detroit on January 6, 1971**

5. Who was the first black star of the famous Ziegfeld Follies?

    a. **Bert Williams**
    b. **Noble Sissle**
    c. **Ina Mae McKinley**
    d. **Iva Anderson**

6. What was the first show that featured black female singers?

    a. ***Tan Terrific*, produced in Boston in 1902**
    b. ***Rock 'em, Sock 'em*, produced in Washington, D.C., in 1912**
    c. ***Harlem Review*, produced in New York in 1897**
    d. ***Creole Show*, produced in Boston in 1891**

7. In what year was Scott Joplin's opera *Treemonisha* composed?

    a. **1912**
    b. **1915**
    c. **1902**
    d. **1922**

8. Who was the first black star to costar in a continuing TV series?

   a. Sammy Davis, Jr. **c. Bill Cosby**
   b. Flip Wilson **d. Gregory Morris**

9. What do Bill Cosby, Godfrey Cambridge, Dick Gregory, Flip Wilson and Richard Pryor have in common?

   a. They are all famous comedians
   b. They all live in Hollywood
   c. They all own Mark IVs
   d. They all have produced their own movies

10. Who was the first black female to compete in the Miss America beauty pageant?

   a. Janet M. Horton **c. Joyce H. Hill**
   b. Julia M. Agnew **d. Cheryl A. Browne**

---

1. Dean Dixon 2. Roland Hayes 3. George W. Chadwick's Second Symphony in 1886 4. the Dance Theater of Harlem 5. Bert Williams 6. Creole Show, in Boston, in 1891 7. 1915 8. Bill Cosby costarred with Robert Culp in "I Spy." He received the Emmy Award for it in 1965 9. They are all famous comedians 10. Cheryl A. Browne

---

ENTERTAINMENT QUIZ 4

Match the following with the correct paragraph. There are twelve possible answers but only ten paragraphs. Some answers may be used more than once.

Dizzy Gillespie
Robert Lancaster
Charlie Parker
Wes Montgomery
John Lewis
Huddie Ledbetter (Leadbelly)
Sidney Catlett
Charles "Buddy" Bolden
Louis Armstrong
Harry Carney
Duke Ellington
Count Basie

1. He was largely responsible for revolutionizing the art of black musical improvisation.

2. He was generally regarded as "The World's Greatest Jazz Guitarist."

3. He was known as "King of the 12 String Guitarists."

4. He was one of the best known and greatest jazz drummers of the 1930s and '40s.

5. He is thought to have organized the first jazz band in the U.S.

6. He was an outstanding jazz musician whose trumpet style influenced trumpeters during the 1920s and '30s.

7. He is known as the first and greatest performer of jazz on the baritone saxophone.

8. His first record hit was released in 1930. It was originally titled "Dreamy Blues," later changed to "Mood Indigo."

9. He is generally regarded as the leader of the best jazz band in the U.S. today.

10. He became internationally known as the arranger, conductor, composer and pianist for a group called the Modern Jazz Quartet (MJQ).

1. *Charlie Parker* 2. *Wes Montgomery* 3. *Huddie (Leadbelly) Ledbetter* 4. *Sidney Catlett* 5. *Charles "Buddy" Bolden* 6. *Louis Armstrong* 7. *Harry Carney* 8. *Duke Ellington* 9. *Count Basie* 10. *John Lewis*

ENTERTAINMENT QUIZ 5

Match the following with the correct paragraph. There are twelve possible answers but only ten paragraphs. Some answers may be used more than once.

Ira Aldridge	**Cleon Thompson**
Arthur Mitchell	**Leroy Butcher**
William Grant Still	**Paul Robeson**
J. P. Johnson	**Richard B. Harrison**
Dean Dixon	**Lillian O. McCall**
Leontyne Price	**Rember Burthey**

1. She was the first black operatic star to sing a leading role on television.

2. He was the first black to play Shakespearean characters. He was educated at the African Free School in New York in the early 1800s.

3. He was the first great black actor in the U.S. He made his acting debut while in his teens with an all-black cast in New York in Sheridan's *Pizzarro.*

4. He was the first black to conduct the New York Philharmonic Orchestra. Harlem-born, he returned to the U.S. in 1970 after holding positions in Sweden and Germany and conducting nearly every major symphony in Europe.

5. He was the first black conductor to lead a major symphony orchestra. He led the Los Angeles Symphony Orchestra as a guest conductor in the Hollywood Bowl in 1936.

6. He was famous as a singer, actor and athlete. His first fame came as an athlete at Rutgers University. He was valedictorian of his graduating class, a Phi Beta Kappa and a Broadway star.

7. He gained national prominence on the basis of one role, "De Lawd," in *Green Pastures.* His first performance was on February 26, 1930.

8. He was a famed jazz pianist who wrote a symphony titled *Symphony Harlem* in 1932.

9. She sang the leading operatic role at the opening of the Metropolitan Opera at Lincoln Center in New York on September 16, 1966. She is known as the "Voice of the Century."

10. He was the first black ballet star to become a member of a major ballet company.

---

1. Leontyne Price 2. Ira Aldridge 3. Ira Aldridge 4. Dean Dixon
5. William Grant Still 6. Paul Robeson 7. Richard B. Harrison
8. J. P. Johnson 9. Leontyne Price 10. Arthur Mitchell

ENTERTAINMENT QUIZ 6

Match the following with the correct paragraph. There are twelve possible answers but only ten paragraphs. Some answers may be used more than once.

Duke Ellington	**Louis Jordan**
Art Tatum	**Fletcher Henderson**
Mamie Smith	**W. C. Handy**
Thomas "Fats" Waller	**James P. Johnson**
Coleman Hawkins	**"King" Oliver**
James P. Jones	**Shep Fields**

1. He was seventeen years old when he composed his first piece of music, "Soda Fountain Rag."

2. He was the classically trained jazz pianist with the unique technique that established a new school of piano soloists.

3. Born in 1899, he was an orchestra leader, pianist, composer of national and international fame.

4. He was the first jazz pianist to record a jazz piano solo, the "Carolina Shout," for Okeh Records in 1921.

5. He was the first jazz musician to gain fame on the saxophone. In 1939, his recording of "Body and Soul" made him famous.

6. He was the first bandleader to become famous playing jazz.

7. He is known as "The Father of the Blues." He composed the famous "St. Louis Blues" as well as countless other highly successful songs.

8. He was the first jazz musician to use the organ as a jazz instrument.

9. The first authentic blues recording ("Crazy Blues") was made by her.

10. His jazz band was the first to record on a major record label.

---

1. Duke Ellington 2. Art Tatum 3. Duke Ellington 4. James P. Johnson 5. Coleman Hawkins 6. Fletcher Henderson 7. W. C. Handy 8. Thomas "Fats" Waller 9. Mamie Smith 10. "King" Oliver, in 1923

Invention, Exploration and Discovery

As we go about our daily business, there are many things that influence the manner in which we communicate with friends and acquaintances. Did you know that a black man who worked with Thomas Edison and Alexander Graham Bell drew up the plans for Bell's first telephone? If you did, you are probably among a fortunate few who possess such knowledge. It is a fact that has not been well publicized. All we usually hear of is Bell's contribution.

There are countless inventions by blacks and they cover everything from food processing to electrical technology. Granville T. Woods had more than sixty patents in electrical development before his death in 1910. The inventions by blacks point out the contributions that blacks have made to the comfort and advancement of mankind.

INVENTION, EXPLORATION AND DISCOVERY QUIZ 1

1. Who invented water closets (toilets) for railway cars on February 10, 1900?

   a. Latimer and Brown **c. Lee and Guest**
   b. Blair and Helm **d. Robertson and Jones**

2. Who invented the striking clock?

   a. Matt Henson in 1787 **c. Benjamin Banneker in 1761**
   b. Nat Thurman in 1784 **d. Nathaniel Dett in 1761**

3. Which of the following were invented and patented by blacks?

   a. horseshoe, lawnmower and golf tee
   b. bottle cap, pencil sharpener and fountain pen
   c. folding chair, elevator, refrigerator, clothes dryer and automatic stop light
   d. all of the above

4. Who invented the machine for picking cotton?

   a. A. P. Albert of Louisiana
   b. G. F. Grant of Arkansas
   c. S. L. Dickerson of Kentucky
   d. J. P. Blake of Texas

5. Who invented the player piano machinery?

   a. J. H. Dickinson and S. L. Dickinson
   b. R. M. Jackson and M. J. Jackson
   c. W. U. Moore and E. T. Moore
   d. O. J. Henry and B. V. Henry

6. Who invented the golf tee?

   a. **George H. Freeman**
   b. **George F. Grant**
   c. **George W. Martin**
   d. **George M. Silver**

7. Who invented the first practical refrigerator system for trucks and railroad freight cars?

   a. **Kenneth Spann of Detroit**
   b. **Frederick M. Jones of Detroit**
   c. **Emmitt Long of Philadelphia**
   d. **Clarence Laster of Philadelphia**

8. Who "invented" ice cream?

   a. **William King**
   b. **Harts Brown**
   c. **Leon Wiggins**
   d. **Augustus Jackson**

9. Who invented the first corn harvester?

   a. **Henry Blair**
   b. **Andrew Moore**
   c. **Herbert Brantley**
   d. **James Crawford**

10. It was not until some time after the emancipation of slaves that blacks were allowed to obtain patents for their inventions. Who was the first black man to secure a patent for his invention?

    a. **George Washington Carver, for his method of extracting minerals from peanuts**
    b. **Henry Blair, for his seed-cultivator**
    c. **William Ballow, for his hat rack**
    d. **Tony Helm, for his all-angle wrench**

1. Latimer and Brown 2. Benjamin Banneker 3. all of the above 4. A. P. Albert of Louisiana 5. J. H. Dickinson and S. L. Dickinson 6. George F. Grant 7. Frederick M. Jones 8. Augustus Jackson 9. Henry Blair 10. Henry Blair

INVENTION, EXPLORATION AND DISCOVERY QUIZ 2

1. True/False The first clock made entirely in America was constructed by Benjamin Banneker, who had never seen a clock before. It continued to run accurately, striking all hours regularly for twenty years.

2. True/False In 1858, Jeremiah S. Black, attorney general of the U.S., ruled that since slaves were not citizens, they could not be granted patents. Jo Anderson, a slave on the plantation of Cyrus McCormick, made a major contribution to McCormick's grain harvester, popularly called "McCormick's Reaper."

3. True/False A paper cutter similar to those used on wax paper and aluminum foil boxes was invented by William B. Purvis of Philadelphia in 1884.

4. True/False Benjamin Banneker is credited with inventing a casket-lowering device.

5. True/False The same person who invented horseshoes (James Ricks) also invented "overshoes for horses."

6. True/False T. J. Bird was the inventor of an apparatus for detaching horses from carriages.

7. True/False The cooker (oil heater) that is widely used by hunters was invented by Simeon Newson of Detroit.

8. True/False The patent holder for a spring seat for chairs and cash carriers belonged to A. B. Blackburn.

9. True/False In some instances, slaves were granted patent rights but earned little if any royalties.

10. True/False The velocipede (which today is called the tricycle) was invented by a black craftsman named Johnson.

---

1. True 2. True 3. True 4. False 5. True 6. True 7. True 8. True 9. False 10. True

---

INVENTION, EXPLORATION AND DISCOVERY QUIZ 3

Match the inventions with the inventor.

Inventions	Scrambled Clues
1. railway signal	A. B. Blackburn
2. eggbeater	Peter Walker
3. railway safety switch	J. R. Winter
4. car wash	Benjamin Montgomery
5. folding chair	W. H. Phelps
6. boat propeller	W. Johnson
7. grass catcher	W. H. Jackson
8. fire escape ladder	Purdy and Sadgwar
9. bait holder for fishermen	H. Peterson
10. machine for cleaning seed cotton	Peter Walker

---

1. A. B. Blackburn 2. W. Johnson 3. W. H. Jackson 4. W. H. Phelps 5. Purdy and Sadgwar 6. Benjamin Montgomery 7. H. Peterson 8. J. R. Winter 9. Peter Walker 10. Peter Walker

---

INVENTION, EXPLORATION AND DISCOVERY QUIZ 4

Match the inventions with the inventor.

Inventions

1. milk bottle opener and bottle cover
2. machine for making paper bags
3. automatic railroad car coupling device
4. churn (for churning milk) and can for insect spray
5. horseshoes
6. detachable mop handle and disposable mop
7. gas heater and clothes dryer
8. street sweeper
9. reins-holding device for horses
10. oil heater (cooker)

Scrambled Clues

Richard B. Spikes
William B. Purvis
Andrew J. Beard
Simeon Newson
T. J. Bird
A. C. Richardson
James Ricks
Thomas S. Stewart
B. F. Jackson
Charles B. Brooks

---

1. Richard B. Spikes 2. William B. Purvis 3. Andrew J. Beard 4. A. C. Richardson 5. James Ricks 6. Thomas S. Stewart 7. B. F. Jackson 8. Charles B. Brooks 9. T. J. Bird 10. Simeon Newson

---

INVENTION, EXPLORATION AND DISCOVERY QUIZ 5

Match the inventions with the inventor.

Inventions	Scrambled Clues
1. electric railway	Elijah McCoy
2. potato chip	W. B. Purvis
3. toggle harpoon (used in whaling)	Huram S. Thomas
4. self-setting animal trap	Elijah McCoy
5. steam lubricator, lawn sprinkler, and steam dome	Lewis Temple
6. folding ironing table	W. S. Campbell
7. two-cycle gasoline engine	Frederick McKinley Jones
8. sending and receiving sets for helmets of football players	B. V. Montez
9. potato digger	P. D. Smith
10. plans for Bell's first telephone	Lewis Latimer

---

1. W. B. Purvis 2. Huram S. Thomas 3. Lewis Temple 4. W. S. Campbell 5. Elijah McCoy 6. Elijah McCoy 7. Frederick McKinley Jones 8. B. V. Montez 9. P. D. Smith 10. Lewis Latimer

---

INVENTION, EXPLORATION AND DISCOVERY QUIZ 6

Match the following with the correct paragraph. There are twelve possible answers but only ten paragraphs. Some answers may be used more than once.

David G. Blake	**Norbert Rilleaux**
Adolpus Samms	**Henry Boyd**
Emmanuel M. Moore	**W. H. Richardson**
Elbert R. "Doc" Robertson	**Garrett A. Morgan**
Granville T. Woods	**Dr. Lloyd A. Hall**
Harold Floyd	**Michael Smothers**

1. He invented the chilled groove wheel used by all railroads. Although it was patented, he maintained that it had been stolen by a white man who sold it to the Chicago Railway Company. In a lengthy legal battle, the U.S. Supreme Court decided in his favor and awarded him $13,000,000 in royalties. He died in 1925.

2. He was from Baltimore, Maryland, and received patent numbers 405,599 and 405,600 for his invention of a child's carriage (baby carriage).

3. He is a black U.S. Army sergeant and developed an "air frame center support" using an engineering concept which eliminates the second- and third-stage engines from multi-stage rockets, thus making greater payloads possible.

4. He invented a machine that produced rails (bedsteads) for beds. He had to obtain a patent in the name of a white man. He built a factory to produce the rails that employed twenty to fifty workmen. It was damaged several times by arsonists and finally was destroyed.

5. Over eighty patents were issued to him for his meat-curing salt formulas which revolutionized the meat-curing industry.

6. He (1806–1894) was a famous inventor and engineer. He reduced the cost of granulated sugar in 1840 by inventing a vacuum pan that revolutionized refining techniques. He also designed a method for handling sewage which could have removed the menace of yellow fever from New Orleans, but his scheme was not adopted.

7. He (1856–1910) was an inventor of electrical appliances. In Cincinnati, Ohio, he opened a factory for the manufacture of telephone, telegraph and electrical equipment. In 1844 he introduced his first invention, a steam-boiler furnace. His most famous invention is the automatic air brake. He patented more than fifteen devices for use in electric railways and a number of telegraphic devices for transmitting messages between moving trains.

8. He designed an earth-moving machine with a capacity for scooping and side-delivering an average of 600 yards of dirt per hour, twice as fast as most dragline machines used by excavators.

9. The gas mask of World War I was based on a device invented by him. In 1916, an explosion below Lake Erie trapped more than twenty men in one of the tunnels of the Cleveland Waterworks. Intense smoke and gas made rescue attempts impossible. Eventually someone remembered that the inventor had been trying to find a manufacturer for his gas inhalator. With his brother and two volunteers, he entered the tunnel with the inhalators and brought up almost all of the workmen. His heroic and dramatic act led to keen interest in the inhalator. The invention was transformed into a gas mask in World War I.

10. He was known in the electrical industry as the "Black Edison" because of his many inventions and great contributions in the area of electrical development. In all, he had more than sixty patents when he died in 1910. Among his inventions are: steam-boiler furnace, automatic air-brake system for railroad trains, telephone transmitter, overhead conducting system for electric railways, the electric incubator, a relay instrument, an electromechanical brake, an automatic safety cut-out for electric circuits (circuit breakers), a type of tunnel construction for electric railways and a galvanic battery.

---

1. Elbert R. "Doc" Robertson 2. W. H. Richardson 3. Adolphus Samms 4. Henry Boyd 5. Dr. Lloyd A. Hall 6. Norbert Rillieux 7. Granville T. Woods 8. Emmanuel M. Moore 9. Garrett A. Morgan 10. Granville T. Woods

---

INVENTION, EXPLORATION AND DISCOVERY QUIZ 7

Match the following with the correct paragraph. There are twelve possible answers but only ten paragraphs. Some answers may be used more than once.

Benjamin Banneker	**G. W. Murry**
Elijah McCoy	**Joseph Stills**
H. Grenon	**Frederick McKinley Jones**
Jan Ernst Matzeliger	**W. B. Purvis**
D. E. Howard	**Garrett A. Morgan**
Franklin Swacker	**Rudolph Brewington**

1. He (1731–1805) was an inventor, astronomer, mathematician, writer of the first almanac and was appointed by George Washington as one of the planners of the city of Washington.

2. He (1852–1899) invented the shoe-lasting machine (for attaching soles on shoes) in Lynn, Massachusetts, on March 20, 1883. His invention revolutionized the shoe industry. With his invention, shoes were made in half the time. It helped make Lynn the shoe capital of the world.

3. On January 24, 1939, he received a patent for his invention of an optical apparatus for indicating the position of a tool.

4. He (1875–1963) was the inventor of the first automatic stop signal (traffic light). He was born in Paris, Tennessee, during the Reconstruction period. He also invented a belt fastener for sewing machines. He sold the patent rights to his stop signal for $40,000.

5. On June 5, 1894, he was awarded six patents for his inventions of a planter, a cotton chopper, a fertilizer distributor, a combined cottonseed planter and a fertilizer distributor–reaper.

6. He (1844–1928) received over fifty-seven patents for his inventions from 1872 to 1920. His inventions included automatic lubricating appliances and other devices pertaining to telegraphy and electricity. He is also acredited with inventing lubricating systems for railroad cars.

7. He was awarded patent No. 419,065 for his invention of the fountain pen. He held sixteen different patents for bag fasteners, hand stamps, paper bag machines, electric railway, electric railway switch and a magnetic car and balancing device.

8. From Detroit, Michigan, he received patent No. 361,435 for his invention of the lubricator attachment. A visible feed glass made it possible to see when oil was to be added for lubrication of machines — an integral part of his famous drip-cup lubricating system.

9. He was granted patent No. 554,867 on February 18, 1896, by the United States Patent Office for his razor-stropping device. Like many black men of his era, he became a skilled laborer during slavery, which was abolished during his lifetime.

10. He invented a refrigeration unit for trucks which resulted in the creation of new markets for many food crops and made frozen foods available to more people. His invention also led to the creation of a firm called Thermo King, of Minneapolis, Minnesota.

1. Benjamin Banneker 2. Jan Ernst Matzeliger 3. D. E. Howard 4. Garrett A. Morgan 5. G. W. Murry 6. Elijah McCoy 7. W. B. Purvis 8. Elijah McCoy 9. H. Grenon 10. Frederick McKinley Jones

INVENTION, EXPLORATION AND DISCOVERY QUIZ 8

Match the following with the correct paragraph. There are twelve possible answers but only ten paragraphs. Some answers may be used more than once.

Estevancio (Little Stephen)	**Lloyd Augustus Hall**
Harold D. West	**James P. Beckwourth**
Andrew J. Barnes	**Ernest E. Just**
Percy L. Julian	**Jean Baptiste Point du Sable**
Matthew Henson	**Robert H. Lawrence**
George Washington Carver	**Jake Terrell**

1. He was the first black astronaut chosen to make a journey to the moon. He had a doctoral degree in chemistry and would have made one of the first lunar trips, but he died in the crash of an Air Force F-104 jet at Edwards Air Force Base, California, in 1968.

2. He was the first man to reach the North Pole (1909). He arrived a bit ahead of Commodore Robert E. Peary and raised the American flag there.

3. In 1538, he led an expedition of four hundred from Mexico into the territory of the American Southwest. He is credited with the discovery of what is today Arizona and New Mexico.

4. He discovered a pass through the Sierra Nevada Mountains that bears his name. He was an explorer, mountain man and fur trader. His pass became a trail that was to carry numerous settlers from Reno, Nevada, to the California border.

5. He was the first permanent settler in Chicago. He built a cabin at the mouth of the Chicago River in about 1790. His trading post spread out to include a forty-foot house, lakehouse, dairy, smokehouse, workshop, stable and barn.

6. He was the first biologist to receive the Spingarn Medal. He received distinction in his field through his research on egg fertilization and the functioning of cells.

7. He was chief chemist and director of research for Griffith Laboratories of Chicago. He revolutionized the meat-packing industry with his discoveries of curing salts for the preserving and processing of meats. He holds more than twenty-five patents for the processing and packaging of food products, especially meats and bakery products.

8. He developed many products from the peanut, the sweet potato and the soybean and changed the economy of the South by freeing it from dependence on cotton. The Department of Agriculture published his ideas for farmers all over the world.

9. He was regarded as the world's foremost producer of synthetic steroid drugs from the soybean. He held more than eighty patents, including those for the synthesis of progesterone, estrone and testosterone hormones from plants.

10. He was the first person to synthesize the amino acid threonine in the laboratory.

---

1. Major Robert H. Lawrence 2. Matthew Henson 3. Estevancio (Little Stephen) 4. James P. Beckworth 5. Jean Baptiste Point du Sable 6. Ernest E. Just 7. Lloyd Augustus Hall 8. George Washington Carver 9. Percy L. Julian 10. Harold D. West

---

Labor

The sit-ins of the 1960s and the resultant opening of public accommodations and jobs gave rise to a new economic status for many blacks. Prior to the enactment of the Economic Opportunity Act of 1964, the majority of blacks saw little opportunity for employment in middle and top management positions in industrial organizations and governmental agencies. This is not to say that all is well on the labor front today. However, it is meant to imply that employment opportunities have increased since the civil rights movement of the early 1960s.

Writers like Michael Harrington and James Baldwin helped bring a deeper appreciation for the problems facing blacks on the labor front. Harrington's book *The Other America* brought attention to poverty in the United States and focused on the plight of poor people. Baldwin helped us understand what it meant to be black in a morally bankrupt affluent society.

One of the major problems confronting blacks, where jobs are concerned, is the refusal and reluctance of labor unions to admit them into their ranks. The white unions control most building trades and manufacturing concerns and have systematically excluded black applicants from gaining entry. As a result, blacks began to form their own unions in the last half of the nineteenth and early part of the twentieth century.

Because of the widespread discrimination in employment, the federal government had to intervene on behalf of racial minorities across the country. Legislation such as Title VII of the Civil Rights Act of 1964 challenged the racist practices of labor unions. Today, most state governments have adopted equal employment opportunity policies.

LABOR QUIZ 1

1. True/False President Roosevelt's Executive Order 8802 issued in 1941 declared that the official policy of the U.S. was to prohibit racial discrimination in employment. It is considered the first "labor law" of the U.S. that involved black citizens.

2. True/False Asa Philip Randolph is noted for his civil rights leadership. He is also known as the "elder statesman" among civil rights leaders. He was head of the Brotherhood of Automobile Workers for several years.

3. True/False Title VII of the Civil Rights Act of 1964 involves a realistic basis of judging repeated claims about "great progress" in eliminating racist practices within organized labor.

4. True/False About half of all black teenagers are in school; of those out of school, over one third are not in the labor force.

5. True/False The first black labor union, the Colored National Labor Union, was formed in Washington, D.C. Its members were urged to set up cooperatives and loan associations and to purchase land.

6. True/False The first Convention of Black Labor was held in the United States in 1969.

7. True/False Labor Day was originated by a black man.

8. True/False Labor unions became the first major American organizations in the post–Civil War period to exclude blacks.

9. True/False Black men were less likely to be in the labor force than white men until the late 1960s, when black rates started to increase.

10. True/False Black unemployment is usually highest in the northeastern states and lowest in the north-central and western states.

---

1. True 2. False 3. True 4. True 5. True 6. False. It was held in 1869 7. True. In 1890, John P. Green, a state representative in Ohio, introduced a bill to create Labor Day 8. True 9. False — just the opposite is true 10. False — just the opposite is true

---

LABOR QUIZ 2

1. He was born in 1899, is vice president of the AFL-CIO and was one of the organizers of the March on Washington in 1941 that led to the formation of the Fair Employment Compensation Practice Policy. He was also the first president of the Brotherhood of Sleeping Car Porters.

   a. Willard Townsend **c. David G. Blake**
   b. A. Philip Randolph **d. Lovell Jones**

2. Which state initiated the first state Fair Employment Practice Agency?

   a. Illinois **c. Michigan**
   b. New York **d. Ohio**

3. Who threatened a march on Washington that led to the barring of discrimination in defense work during World War II?

   a. Philip Murry
   b. Martin Luther King, Jr.
   c. James Farmer
   d. A. Philip Randolph

4. An attempt to organize blacks into union membership (and discourage the use of blacks as strikebreakers) was made in 1925 by:

   a. the American Federation of Labor (AFL)
   b. the Urban League
   c. the Brotherhood of Sleeping Car Porters
   d. American Negro Labor Congress

5. The Brotherhood of Sleeping Car Porters and Maids was organized in 1925 by:

   a. Willard Townsend **c. Sidney A. Martin**
   b. Harland Randolph **d. A. Philip Randolph**

6. When did the U.S. Civil Service Commission eliminate racial designations on employees' personnel forms?

   a. February, 1947 **c. February, 1967**
   b. February, 1957 **d. February, 1960**

7. In America's twenty largest standard metropolitan statistical areas (SMAs) black unemployment has traditionally been lowest in:

   a. northeastern states **c. southeastern states**
   b. southwestern states **d. north-central states**

8. Of the following cities, which one usually has the highest percentage of blacks gainfully employed?

   a. San Francisco **c. Cleveland**
   b. Houston **d. Detroit**

9. Dr. Martin Luther King, Jr., was assassinated while helping to mobilize sanitation workers in:

   a. Memphis **c. Cleveland**
   b. St. Louis **d. Nashville**

10. Who is the author of the following:

    "The AFL-CIO is for civil rights — without reservation and without delay. The labor movement is dedicated to those truths that were self-evident to the authors of the Declaration of Independence . . . Unfortunately, to the shame of the nation, discrimination still exists. It must be wiped out if the United States is to be truly the champion of freedom in a world where non-whites are an overwhelming majority."

a. **Abram Harris**
b. **George Meany**
c. **John L. Lewis**
d. **Walter Reuther**

---

1. A. Philip Randolph 2. New York 3. A. Philip Randolph 4. the Urban League 5. A. Philip Randolph 6. February, 1957 7. north-eastern states 8. San Francisco 9. Memphis, Tennessee 10. George Meany

---

Literature

Many writers have taken it upon themselves to let the world know how they feel about certain aspects of American life or life in general. They have written both fiction and non-fiction books, poetry, plays and songs. Some of them have chosen to write books about the black man's struggle in America, while others preferred to write inspirational poems and songs depicting the beauty that life has to offer if we would only look to see it and touch to feel it.

The lyrics to "Lift Every Voice and Sing" are inspiring, to say the least, and they portray a picture of great hope for mankind. Although freedom appears to be the major theme, an underlying theme of equal importance is love and bringing people together so they might sing of the day when victory over oppression is achieved.

The world owes a great debt to many black writers for their contribution to the literary world. Carter G. Woodson was not only a historian, he was a great black historian who is considered to be the "Father of Negro History." Prior to his time, historical records relating to black life were not a prime concern of writers of historically oriented books on the American experience. Langston Hughes, James Weldon Johnson and Paul Laurence Dunbar are black men who have made great literary contributions and whose lives have enriched mankind. They were not alone. Others (past and present) have made outstanding contributions in the field of literature. A few are "sampled" here.

LITERATURE QUIZ 1

1. In what year did the first novel written by a black man appear in the U.S.?

   a. 1881 **c. 1853**
   b. 1876 **d. 1823**

2. In what year was the first history of the black American written in the U.S.?

   a. in 1863 by W. E. B. Du Bois
   b. in 1841 by James Pennington
   c. in 1875 by Daniel Alexander
   d. in 1870 by Robert M. Blake

3. In what year did the first black history *textbook* appear in the U.S.?

   a. 1865 **c. 1841**
   b. 1880 **d. 1870**

4. What is the title of the "Negro National Anthem"?

   a. **"We Shall Overcome"**
   b. **"Lift Every Voice and Sing"**
   c. **"Swing Low Sweet Chariot"**
   d. **"Go Down Moses"**

5. What do the following blacks have in common? Jean Toomer, Walter White, Wallace Thurman, Jesse Fauset, Rudolph Fisher, Nella Larsen, Alain Locke, Charles S. Johnson and William Stanley Braithwaite.

   a. **They were all writers and critics during the Negro Renaissance that began in Harlem in 1922**
   b. **They were all editors of *Crisis* magazine, the official journal of the NAACP, at one time or another**
   c. **They were all members of the original founding group of the NAACP**
   d. **They were all elected to the black writers' Hall of Fame**

6. Where was Phillis Wheatley, the famous black poetess, born?

   a. **United States**
   b. **Africa**
   c. **Jamaica**
   d. **Barbados**

7. What do the following blacks have in common? Hale Woodruff, Elizabeth Prophet, Selma Burke, Sargent Johnson, Richmond Barthe, Jacob Lawrence, Charles Alston, Ernest Crichlow, Romare Bearden and E. Simms Campbell.

   a. **They are (or were) all leading artists**
   b. **They are (or were) all leading writers**
   c. **They are (or were) leading musicians**
   d. **They are (or were) leading undertakers**

8. Who is the author of the following books? *The Fire Next Time, Another Country* and *Tell Me How Long the Train's Been Gone.*

   a. James Baldwin **c. Arna Bontemps**
   b. Malachi Greene **d. Eldridge Cleaver**

9. He was one of the most productive writers of the twentieth century. He was born in Alexandria, Louisiana, in 1902. Among his numerous works are: *We Have Tomorrow, Sad-Faced Boy, Any Place But Here* and *Great Slave Narratives.* He is:

   a. Claude Brown **c. Sterling Brown**
   b. Arna Bontemps **d. Arthur P. Davis**

10. He is considered by many critics to be one of the most articulate novelists today. His first novel was *Youngblood* (1954). Among his other publications are: *And Then We Heard the Thunder, Odds Against Tomorrow* (screenplay) and *Blackman's Burden.* He is:

   a. John O. Killens **c. Thornell F. Page**
   b. Hugh J. Scott **d. Russell L. Adams**

---

1. 1853 2. 1841 by James Pennington 3. 1841 4. "Lift Every Voice and Sing" 5. They were all writers and critics during the Negro Renaissance that began in Harlem in 1922 6. Africa 7. They are all leading artists 8. James Baldwin 9. Arna Bontemps 10. John O. Killens

---

LITERATURE QUIZ 2

The following are excerpts from the writings of some notable blacks. Identify the person who wrote:

1. "We want our freedom now: we want it all; we want it here!"

   a. Cleveland L. Robinson
   b. Martin Luther King, Jr.
   c. George C. Dumas
   d. Edmund C. Weaver

2. "To those of my race who depend upon bettering their condition in a foreign land or who underestimate the importance of cultivating friendly relations with the Southern white man, who is his next door neighbor, I say 'Cast down your bucket where you are'—cast it down in making friends in every manly way of the people of all races by whom we are surrounded. Cast it down in agriculture, mechanics, in commerce, in domestic service, and in the professions."

   a. W. E. B. Du Bois
   b. James C. Cheek
   c. Benjamin E. Mays
   d. Booker T. Washington

3. "Be proud my Race, in Mind and soul;
   Thy name is writ on Glory's scroll
   In Characters of fire,
   High 'mid the clouds of fame's bright sky
   Thy banners' blazoned folds now fly,
   And truth shall lift them higher."

a. **Paul Laurence Dunbar**
b. **Rayford Logan**
c. **Countee Cullen**
d. **Sylvester Simms**

4. "There is no defense or security for any of us except in the highest intelligence and development of all."

a. **W. E. B. Du Bois** c. **Jesse B. Blayton**
b. **Clarence A. Guest** d. **Booker T. Washington**

5. "Our students have come to understand that whereas they marched and talked loudly during the 1960s, today they must stage long, quiet sit-ins in the library and stand-ins in the laboratory if they are to compete in the years that follow."

a. **Milton K. Curry** c. **Elias Blake**
b. **Leroy Miles** d. **George H. Thomas**

6. "Well, son, I'll tell you:
Life for me ain't been no crystal stair.
It's had tacks in it
And splinters
And boards torn up,
And places with no carpet on the floor —
Bare . . ."

a. **Andress Taylor** c. **Langston Hughes**
b. **William Couch** d. **Herb Jeffries**

7. "The history of the black race proves them to be wonderfully adapted to all countries, all climates, and all conditions. Their tenacity of life, their powers of en-

durance, their malleable toughness, would almost imply special inter-position on their behalf. The ten thousand horrors of slavery, striking hard upon the sensitive soul, have bruised and battered and stung, but have not killed. The poor bondman lifts a smiling face above the surface of a sea of agonies, hoping on, hoping ever. His tawny brother, the Indian, dies under the flashing glance of the Anglo-Saxon. Not so the Negro; civilization cannot kill him."

a. Frederick Douglass **c. Angela Davis**
b. Langston Hughes **d. Angela King**

8. "Before the victory's won maybe some more will have to get scarred up, lose jobs, face the problem of being called bad names. Before the victory's won, maybe some more will have to face the tragedy of physical death."

   a. Martin Luther King, Jr.
   b. Frederick Douglass
   c. Ralph Abernathy
   d. Jesse Jackson

9. "Up you mighty race. You can accomplish what you will! Build your future on these foundations: Freedom, Justice and Equality."

   a. Muhammad Ali **c. Leroy Dues**
   b. Elijah Muhammad **d. Lloyd Cofer**

10. "Freedom is never voluntarily given by the oppressor; it must be demanded by the oppressed."

   a. Martin Luther King, Jr.
   b. Whitney Young, Jr.
   c. H. Rap Brown
   d. Stokely Carmichael

1. Martin Luther King, Jr. 2. Booker T. Washington 3. Paul Laurence Dunbar 4. Booker T. Washington 5. Milton K. Curry 6. Langston Hughes 7. Frederick Douglass 8. Martin Luther King, Jr. 9. Elijah Muhammad 10. Martin Luther King, Jr.

LITERATURE QUIZ 3

The following are excerpts from the writings of some notable blacks. Identify the person who wrote:

1. "The problem of the twentieth century is the color line — the relation of the darker to the lighter races of men in Asia and Africa, in America and the islands of the sea."

   a. George Washington Carver
   b. Lester B. Granger
   c. Marcus Garvey
   d. W. E. B. Du Bois

2. "Democracy is the most used term in the world today. But some of its uses are abuses. Everybody says 'Democracy!' but everybody has his own definition. By the extraordinary weight of the Presidency of the United States many undemocratic people have had this word forced upon their lips but have not yet had the right ideal forced upon their hearts."

   a. William Pickens
   b. William Crisp
   c. William Purvis
   d. William Jones

3. "I have a dream that one day this nation will rise up and live out the true meaning of its creed: 'We hold these truths to be self-evident; that all men are created equal.'

   I have a dream that one day on the red hills of Georgia the sons of former slaves and the sons of former slave owners will be able to sit down together at the table of brotherhood.

   I have a dream that one day even the state of Mississippi, a state sweltering with the heat of oppression, will be transformed into an oasis of freedom and justice.

   I have a dream that my little children will one day live in a nation where they will not be judged by the color of their skin but by the content of their character . . ."

   a. W. E. B. Du Bois
   b. Martin Luther King, Jr.
   c. Adam Clayton Powell, Jr.
   d. Charles C. Diggs

4. "Islam dignifies the black man, and it gives him the desire to be clean, internally and externally, and to have for the first time a sense of dignity."

a. **Elijah Muhammad**
b. **Malcolm X**
c. **Lonnie Shabazz**
d. **Muhammad Ali**

5. "Shout, O children!
   Shout, you're free.
   For God has brought you liberty!"

   a. **W. E. B. Du Bois**
   b. **Booker T. Washington**
   c. **Marcus Garvey**
   d. **Benjamin E. Mays**

6. "It is one of the commonplaces of American thought that we have a democracy based upon the free will of the governed. The popular idea of the strength of this democracy is that it is founded upon the fact that every American citizen, through the ballot, is a ruler in his own right; that every citizen of age and outside of jail or the insane asylum has the undisputed right to determine through his vote by what laws he shall be governed and by whom these laws shall be enforced."

   a. **James Weldon Johnson**
   b. **Wesley E. Brown**
   c. **James C. Lightfoot**
   d. **Eugene Hall**

7. "It is a cruel jest to say to a bootless man that he should lift himself by his own bootstraps. It is even worse to tell a man to lift himself by his own bootstraps when somebody is standing on the boot."

   a. **A. Philip Randolph**
   b. **Walter Washington**
   c. **Melvin Washington**
   d. **Martin Luther King, Jr.**

9. "Men we shall have only as we make manhood the object of the work of the schools — intelligence, broad sympathy, knowledge of the world that was and is, and of the relation of men to it — this is the curriculum of that Higher Education which must underlie true life."

a. Lester B. Granger | **c. Walter F. Ford**
b. W. E. B. Du Bois | **d. Henry Eiland**

10. "There is no sense in hate; it comes back to you; therefore, make your history so laudable, magnificent and untarnished, that another generation will not seek to repay your seeds for the sins inflicted upon their father. The bones of injustice have a peculiar way of rising from the tombs to plague and mock the iniquitous."

a. Carl Rowan | **c. William Rasberry**
b. Carl Rolark | **d. Marcus Garvey**

---

1. *W. E. B. Du Bois* **2.** *William Pickens* **3.** *Martin Luther King, Jr.* **4.** *Elijah Muhammad* **5.** *W. E. B. Du Bois* **6.** *James Weldon Johnson* **7.** *Martin Luther King, Jr.* **8.** *Countee Cullen* **9.** *W. E. B. Du Bois* **10.** *Marcus Garvey*

LITERATURE QUIZ 4

The following are excerpts from the writings of some notable blacks. Identify the person who wrote:

1. "Make your own little heaven right here and now. Do it by putting business methods into your farming, by growing things in your garden the year around, by building and keeping attractive and comfortable homes for your children so that they will stay at home and not go to the cities . . . by staying in one place, by getting a good teacher and a good preacher . . . by keeping out of debt, and by cultivating friendly relations with your neighbors both black and white."

   a. Roy Wilkins
   b. Nathaniel Dickens
   c. Booker T. Washington
   d. Frederick Douglass

2. "I want very much to talk with you. About Africa. You see, Mr. Asagai, I am looking for my identity!"

   a. Lorraine Hansberry
   b. Lillian McCall
   c. Minnie Moses
   d. Jessie McFarland

3. "If there is not struggle, there is no progress. Those who profess to favor freedom, and yet deprecate agitation, are men who want crops without plowing up the ground. They want rain without thunder and lightning. They want the ocean without the awful roar of its many waters."

   a. Nat Turner
   b. A. Philip Randolph
   c. Denmark Vesey
   d. Frederick Douglass

4. "The fabric of human rights is never completed — and may its borders never be limited by the rights of one group, one system, or one generation."

   a. Roy Wilkins **c. Walter White**
   b. Hugh J. Scott **d. Andrew Billingsley**

5. "I have known rivers:
   I've known rivers ancient as the world and older than
   the flow of human blood in human veins.
   My soul has grown deep like in the rivers."

   a. Langston Hughes **c. Brad Franklin**
   b. York Campbell **d. Countee Cullen**

6. "A race without authority and power is a race without respect."

   a. Leroy Coleman **c. Daniel Alexander**
   b. Marcus Garvey **d. James Woodruff**

7. "The cost of liberty is less than the price of repression."

   a. W. E. B. Du Bois **c. James Towns**
   b. Clyde Walker **d. James Sheldon**

8. "As a black Christian priest, I reject the integration theory. This is not what it's all about. What it IS all about is the struggle for political power that has been going on between black and white Americans from the time the first black man set his foot on this land. It is a war being waged over the entire country, but not for territorial acquisitions. The uniforms are the colors of our skins. The weapons have been guns, ropes, deceit, economic sanctions, propaganda, espionage, and mass psychology. The whites are trying to maintain the political power over black people that they have always

had in this country. The blacks want to wrest away from the whites what they feel is their rightful share of that political power."

a. Earl G. Graves **c. James Howe**
b. Alvin J. Boutte **d. James Woodruff**

9. "Your country? How came it yours? Before the Pilgrims landed we were here. Here we have brought our three gifts and mingled them with yours: a gift of story and song-soft, stirring melody in an ill-harmonized and unmelodious land; the gift of sweat and brawn to beat back the wilderness, conquer the soil and lay the foundations of this vast economic empire two hundred years earlier than your weak hands could have done it; the third, a gift of the Spirit. Around us the history of the land has centered for thrice a hundred years; out of the nation's heart we have called all that was best to throttle and subdue all that was worst; fire and blood, prayer and sacrifice, have billowed over this people, and they have found peace only in the altars of the God of Right. Nor has our gift of the Spirit been merely passive. Actively we have woven ourselves with the very warp and woof of this nation — we have fought their battles, shared their sorrow, mingled our blood with theirs, and generation after generation have pleaded with a headstrong, careless people to despise not Justice, Mercy, and Truth, least the nation be smitten with a curse. Our song, our toil, our cheer, and warning have been given to this nation in blood-brotherhood. Are not these gifts worth the giving? Is not this work and striving? Would America have been America without her Negro people?"

a. George Washington Carver **c. Louis Graves**
b. W. E. B. Du Bois **d. Langston Hughes**

10. "All I ask is that you respect me as a human being. I am proud to be a black. I am not ashamed of my dark skin. God has given us certain unique qualities and we cherish them just as Englishmen, Frenchmen, Jews, Indians and every other group of common origin cherish theirs."

a. Jackie Robinson **c. Samuel Gravely**
b. Samuel Botts **d. George Askew**

---

1. *Booker T. Washington* 2. *Lorraine Hansberry* 3. *Frederick Douglass* 4. *Roy Wilkins* 5. *Langston Hughes* 6. *Marcus Garvey* 7. *W. E. B. Du Bois* 8. *James Woodruff* 9. *W. E. B. Du Bois* 10. *Jackie Robinson*

LITERATURE QUIZ 5

Read the possible answers and pick the correct ones based on the *descriptions* that follow:

1. **a. Herbert Brantly**
b. James Weldon Johnson
c. Jackie Robinson
d. John James Audubon

He is the author of the autobiography *I Never Had It Made.* He was also the first black man to break the barriers of racial prejudice in modern baseball.

2. **a. Reginald Kilgore**
b. James Weldon Johnson
c. Jonathan Rogers
d. Wardell Lott

He was the author of the lyrics of "Lift Every Voice and Sing." He was also the first black lawyer admitted to the Florida Bar.

3. **a. Richard White**
   b. Richard Russell
   c. Richard Agee
   d. Richard Wright

   He wrote *Native Son,* which became both a Broadway play and a motion picture.

4. **a. Carter G. Woodson**
   b. Scipio Moorehead
   c. William Wells Brown
   d. Thomas A. Farrington

   He was the founder of the Association for the Study of Negro Life and History and is known as the "Father of Negro History."

5. **a. George Wheeler** **c. William Wells Brown**
   b. Lawrence Chambliss **d. James P. Washington**

   In 1858, he wrote *The Escape,* the first play by an American black.

6. **a. Gwendolyn Edwards**
   b. Gwendolyn Brooks
   c. Gwendolyn Stickland
   d. Gwendolyn Bankhead

   She was the first black writer to win a Pulitzer Prize in literature, for her volume *Annie Allen.* Her other books include *Bronzeville Boys and Girls, Selected Poems* and *Riot.* She was named poet laureate of Illinois in 1968.

7. a. **John H. Hillard** c. **John H. Woodson**
   b. **John H. Conyers** d. **John H. Smythe**

   He was the first black artist to become a member of the Philadelphia Academy of Fine Arts. He was also the first black newsboy in the city of Philadelphia.

8. a. **Scipio Moorehead** c. **John H. Smythe**
   b. **Samuel E. Barnes** d. **Grover S. Franklin**

   He was a contemporary of Phyllis Wheatley and is recognized as the first black painter in the U.S. Two of his paintings are *Aurora* and *Damon and Pythias.*

9. a. **Willa M. Jasper** c. **Edmonia Lewis**
   b. **Edmonia Davidson** d. **June Lockheart**

   She was the first American black woman sculptor to achieve distinction.

10. a. **Frances E. Harper** c. **Dorothy Isaac**
    b. **Cleo Johnson** d. **Peggy Hinson**

    She was the first black woman in the U.S. to write a novel and have it published.

---

1. Jackie Robinson 2. James Weldon Johnson 3. Richard Wright 4. Carter G. Woodson 5. William Wells Brown 6. Gwendolyn Brooks 7. John H. Smythe 8. Scipio Moorehead 9. Edmonia Lewis 10. Frances E. Harper

---

LITERATURE QUIZ 6

Read the possible answers and pick the correct ones based on the *descriptions* that follow.

1. a. **Thomas Johnson**
   b. **King V. Cheek**
   c. **Frank Yerby**
   d. **Nathan Hare**

   Born in 1916, he was a prolific writer of romantic historical fiction. Several of his works have been adapted into motion pictures. Among his works are *The Foxes of Harrow* (1946), which became a major Hollywood film, *The Vixens* (1947), *A Woman Called Fancy* (1951) and *The Saracen Blade* (1952).

2. a. **David Walker**
   b. **Bill Lytle**
   c. **Malcolm L. Corrin**
   d. **Robert Freeman**

   On September 28, 1829, this free black published his anti-slavery pamphlet "Appeal."

3. a. **William D. Loyner**
   b. **Morris Turner**
   c. **Carlton P. Irish**
   d. **Verne L. Ashby**

   He is the black cartoonist responsible for the "Wee Pals" comic strip. His work also appears in the *Black World.* His cartoon has been syndicated since 1966 and appears in more than seventy newspapers in the United States and abroad.

4. a. **Henry Ossawa Tanner**
   b. **Jerome W. Carlson**
   c. **William W. Brown**
   d. **Samuel J. Chrisholm**

   He was a world-prominent artist who painted the following: *Daniel in the Lion's Den, Resurrection of Lazarus* and *The Disciples at Emmaus.*

5. a. **Karl Gregory** c. **Roderik Young**
   b. **Lee O. Cherry** d. **Henry O. Tanner**

He was a noted painter whose subject matter ranged widely. He painted scenes of black plantation life, European peasant studies, landscapes, animal pictures and biblical scenes. His works include *The Five Virgins* and *The Return of the Holy Women.*

6. a. **Langston Hughes** c. **James Howe**
   b. **Carl Smith** d. **Lawrence Wright**

He was a famous poet, writer, playwright, historian, a prolific author and a scholar. Among his works are *A Pictorial History of the Negro in America, First Book of Jazz* and *Famous American Negroes.* He was a part of the Harlem Renaissance, and was the "poet laureate" of Harlem.

7. a. **Zora Neale Hurston** c. **Sally Rudine Rundy**
   b. **Helen Major** d. **Evelyn C. Clay**

She was an authority on black folklore and anthropology. Among her works are *Jonah's Gourd Wine, Their Eyes Were Watching God* and *Serapah on the Swanee.*

8. a. **Phillis Wheatley** c. **Edna Bell Thompson**
   b. **Betty Martin** d. **Lucille Davenport**

She was a slave child sold on the docks of Boston in 1761. She achieved international renown as a poet. In 1773, her poems on various subjects were published in London. She was also invited to visit George Washington.

9. a. **William K. Bottsford** c. **William H. Lewis**
   b. **William Wells Bifield** d. **William Wells Brown**

He wrote the first novel by an Afro-American (as an escaped slave) in the U.S. It was titled *Clotel, or the President's Daughter.*

10. a. **Jupiter Harmon** c. **Jupiter Hammon**
    b. **Jupiter Holland** d. **Jupiter Hartman**

He was a Long Island slave and is thought to be the first American black to have a poem printed. It was titled "An Evening Thought: Salvation by Christ with Penitential Cries" (1760).

---

1. Frank Yerby 2. David Walker 3. Morris Turner 4. Henry Ossawa Tanner 5. Henry O. Tanner 6. Langston Hughes 7. Zora Neale Hurston 8. Phillis Wheatley 9. William Wells Brown 10. Jupiter Hammon

---

LITERATURE QUIZ 7

Read the possible answers and pick the correct ones based on the *descriptions* that follow.

1. **a. Lowell Perry** **c. Alexis Haley**
   b. Wilbur Williams **d. Thaddeus Garrett**

   He is an internationally known writer and master story teller. He is the co-author of *The Autobiography of Malcolm X* and recently traced his ancestry back to Africa and has documented it in a book.

2. **a. John Hope Williams** **c. John Hope Watson**
   b. John Hope Franklin **d. John Hope Freeman**

   Born in 1915, he is a historian, educator, Harvard Ph.D., former head of the History Department at Brooklyn College and now a professor of history at the University of Chicago. Among his works are: *From Slavery to Freedom: A History of American Negroes, Reconstruction After the Civil War* and *The Militant South.*

3. **a. James Baldwin** **c. Ralph Ellison**
   b. Frank Yerby **d. Willard Stevens**

   He is the author of *Invisible Man,* which was voted the most distinguished novel of the previous twenty years in a 1965 poll conducted by the New York *Herald Tribune's Book Week.* It won the National Book Award in 1952, the year it was published.

4. a. **Elias J. McFadden** c. **Countee Cullen**
   b. **Leone Bennett, Jr.** d. **Paul Laurence Dunbar**

He (1872–1906) was the first nationally known black poet in the U.S. He was noted for his dialect verse. He died at age 34, beset by tuberculosis, domestic problems and debt.

5. a. **Norman B. Davis** c. **W. E. B. Du Bois**
   b. **Arnold J. McKelvin** d. **Dwight E. Davis**

He (1868–1963) was a black American writer, born in Great Barrington, Massachusetts, educated at Fisk, Harvard and Berlin universities. In 1903, he published *The Souls of Black Folk,* crystallizing his opposition to Booker T. Washington's program of social and political subordination.

6. a. **Les Cenelles** c. **Ralph Ellison**
   b. **Arna W. Bontemps** d. **Willie Swinson**

He was born in 1902, and is an outstanding writer of novels, plays, histories and a compiler of works on blacks. He was a librarian at Fisk University. Among his works are *Story of the Negro, Golden Slippers: An Anthology of Negro Poetry* and *American Heritage.*

7. a. **Leone Bennett, Jr.** c. **Claude McPatter**
   b. **George H. Petty** d. **Sidney Barthwell**

Born in 1928, he is a prolific writer, historian, lecturer and senior editor of *Ebony.* Among his works are *Before the Mayflower: A History of the Negro in America* and *The Shaping of Black America.*

8. a. **Imamu Amiri Baraka** c. **Howard Cameron**
b. **Richard Wright** d. **Leroy Miles**

He is still referred to by some as LeRoi Jones. He is a violent critic of American life and is most insistent in his demands for a separate black culture and aesthetic. He has produced collections of poetry and several plays, including *Dutchman,* which won the Obie Award as best off-Broadway play of 1964.

9. a. **Sterling Brown** c. **Sterling Tucker**
b. **Sterling Moore** d. **Sterling Coates**

He was born in Washington, D.C., in 1901. His first volume of poetry, *Southern Road,* was published in 1932. He is a Harvard University graduate, a prolific author and a retired professor of English at Howard University. He is considered to be one of the finest poets and critics among black American authors.

10. a. ***Les Cenelles*** c. ***Fire and Thunder***
b. ***The Chariot*** d. ***Bye and Bye***

It is the name of the first anthology of black verse in America. It was published in 1845 and contained eighty-two poems by seventeen black poets.

---

1. *Alexis Haley* 2. *John Hope Franklin* 3. *Ralph Ellison* 4. *Paul Laurence Dunbar* 5. *W. E. B. Du Bois* 6. *Arna W. Bontemps* 7. *Leone Bennett, Jr.* 8. *Imamu Amiri Baraka* 9. *Sterling Brown* 10. *Les Cenelles*

Medicine

Dr. Charles Drew died of injuries from an automobile accident that occurred on a North Carolina highway. He might have lived if he had received adequate emergency medical care, but unfortunately he was refused admission to a white hospital because of his skin color. Ironically, the blood volume expander he needed as an aid to survival was his major contribution to the field of medicine.

Dr. Drew, a black man, developed a process for storing blood plasma and has been credited with saving countless lives. There are many other black pioneers in the field of medicine and they run the gamut from researchers to surgeons to nurses. Only a few are recalled here.

MEDICINE QUIZ 1

1. The first training school for black nurses was incorporated in this city in 1891.

   a. Detroit, Michigan
   b. New York, New York
   c. Philadelphia, Pennsylvania
   d. Chicago, Illinois

2. In what year did the American Medical Association seat its first black delegate?

   a. 1958 **c. 1971**
   b. 1950 **d. 1960**

3. What was the first hospital for blacks in the U.S. to be granted a charter (1832)?

   a. North Carolina Infirmary
   b. Alabama Infirmary
   c. Georgia Infirmary
   d. Mississippi Infirmary

4. The Howard University School of Medicine opened its doors with eight students on November 9:

   a. 1863 **c. 1866**
   b. 1868 **d. 1892**

5. In what year was the National Medical Association (NMA) founded?

   a. 1895 **c. 1897**
   b. 1891 **d. 1890**

6. The oldest U.S. black medical association, the Medico-Chirurgical Society, was organized in this city in 1884.

a. **Washington, D.C.**
b. **Chicago, Illinois**
c. **Providence, Rhode Island**
d. **Baltimore, Maryland**

7. Dr. Theodore K. Lawless was most noted for his speciality in:

a. **internal medicine**
b. **dermatology**
c. **surgery**
d. **eye, ear, nose and throat**

8. Who was the black physician who was a pioneer in blood preservation and was founder of the Blood Bank?

a. **Montague Cobb**
b. **John W. Greene**
c. **Charles Drew**
d. **Howard Cameron**

9. Who was the founder of the National Medical Association?

a. **Ernest E. Just**
b. **Edgar A. Love**
c. **Frank M. Snowden**
d. **Henry A. Callis**

10. Who is known as the world expert (and pioneer) researcher in the process of rejection — the action by which the body refuses to accept a transplanted organ?

a. **James Derham**
b. **Samuel L. Kountz**
c. **Daniel Hale Williams**
d. **William Hinton**

---

1. Chicago, Illinois, at the Provident Hospital 2. 1950 3. Georgia Infirmary 4. 1868 5. 1895 6. Washington, D.C. 7. dermatology 8. Charles Drew 9. Henry A. Callis 10. Samuel L. Kountz

---

MEDICINE QUIZ 2

Match the following with the correct paragraph. There are twelve possible answers but only ten paragraphs. Some answers may be used more than once.

Lucas Santomee
Washington, D.C.
Daniel Hale Williams
Mary Eliza Mahomey
James Derham
Provident Hospital
Harold Dadford West
the Vesalius Society
Chicago, Illinois
Peter Murry Marshall
James McCune Smith
the Medico-Chirurgical Society

1. He was the first known black doctor in the U.S. He studied in Holland and practiced under the Dutch and English in the mid-1600s.

2. On January 23, 1891, the first training school for black nurses was founded in this city.

3. It was the first training hospital in Chicago for black doctors and nurses. It was incorporated by Dr. Daniel Hale Williams in 1891.

4. The world's first successful heart operation was performed by him on July 9, 1893.

5. He was the first black president of Meharry Medical College in Nashville. He was a native of Flemington, New Jersey, but grew up in Washington, D.C.

6. He was the first black doctor to practice medicine in New York. He received his degree at the University of Glasgow in Scotland in 1837.

7. It is the name of the oldest black medical society in the United States. It was organized in the District of Columbia on April 24, 1884.

8. She was the first black graduate nurse in the U.S. A family life center is named for her in Boston.

9. He was the first black M.D. to hold a high office in the American Medical Association. He was elected president of the New York County Medical Society on May 24, 1954.

10. He was the first black physician on record who was trained in the U.S. He became an assistant to his master, a doctor. He later won his freedom and set up his own practice.

---

1. Lucas Santomee 2. Chicago, Illinois 3. Provident Hospital 4. Daniel Hale Williams 5. Harold Dadford West 6. James McCune Smith 7. the Medico-Chirurgical Society 8. Mary Eliza Mahoney 9. Peter Murry Marshall 10. James Derham

---

MEDICINE QUIZ 3

Match the following with the correct paragraph. There are twelve possible answers but only ten paragraphs. Some answers may be used more than once.

Dr. David J. Peck	**Dr. Charles Drew**
Dr. William Hinton	**Dr. Daniel Hale Williams**
Dr. Lewis T. Wright	**Dr. William Bentley**
Dr. Elliot C. Roberts	**Dr. Theodore K. Lawless**
Dr. Elbert Robertson	**Dr. Susan McKinney**
Dr. Martin R. Delaney	**Dr. Helen Love**

1. She was the first black woman physician in the U.S. Her practice began in New York City in 1892.
2. He was the first black M.D. to earn a medical degree in the U.S. He earned his degree from Rush Medical College in 1847.
3. He devised a test to determine syphilis.
4. He was the first black professor of medicine at Harvard University. He was also a Harvard graduate.
5. He was the first black admitted to the Harvard University Medical School. He graduated in 1849.
6. He was the first black executive director of the Harlem Hospital. He resigned on July 1, 1972, to become Commissioner of Hospitals in Detroit.
7. The techniques developed by him for separating and preserving blood, as well as his advanced research in the field of blood plasma, helped save countless lives from early World War II to the present.

8. He was one of the leading skin specialists in the United States. He was born in 1892 in Thibodeaux, Louisiana, and was educated at Talladega College in Alabama, the University of Kansas, Columbia and Harvard before receiving his M.D. from Northwestern University.

9. He was the first physician to experiment with aureomycin (an antibiotic) on humans *and* the first black surgeon to be admitted to the American College of Surgeons.

10. He was a world-renowned surgeon and a clinical instructor and demonstrator in anatomy at the Chicago Medical College, where one of his students was Charlie Mayo (of the famous Mayo brothers).

---

1. Dr. Susan McKinney 2. Dr. David J. Peck 3. Dr. William Hinton 4. Dr. William Hinton 5. Dr. Martin R. Delaney 6. Dr. Elliot C. Roberts 7. Dr. Charles Drew 8. Dr. Theodore K. Lawless 9. Dr. Lewis T. Wright 10. Dr. Daniel Hale Williams

---

The Military

The thought of war is not a particularly gratifying one, at least not to rationally thinking men. The destruction it causes is devastating to property and human lives. Yet man has engaged in warfare as far back as memory and historical records take us. Perhaps there are times when good men are forced to go to war to preserve their natural rights as human beings or to help others protect theirs. Blacks have been actively involved in protecting the rights of Americans since and even before the War of 1776. Peter Salem was among the group of Minutemen who responded to the alarm raised by Paul Revere and barred the march of the British Grenadiers on Lexington and Concord on April 19, 1775. Crispus Attucks, a runaway slave, was the first person to be killed by British soldiers in the Revolutionary War. The meritorious service of blacks in the armed forces of the U.S. extends to this day.

MILITARY QUIZ 1

Match the following with the correct paragraph. There are twelve possible answers but only ten paragraphs. Some of the answers may be used more than once.

Major General Frederic E. Davidson
Captain Edward J. Dwight, Jr.
Phyliss Mae Dailey
Spanish-American War
Morgan State and Florida Southern
Howard University and Florida A & M
Lieutenant James Reese Europe
Captain Lloyd Newton
General Daniel C. James
Ensign John W. Lee
Lieutenant Colonel Otis B. Duncan
Alice J. Davenport

1. He was the first black U.S. Army officer to lead an Army division.
2. She was the first black nurse to be sworn into the Navy Nurse Corps.
3. On June 21, 1951, in Korea, the first black to be awarded the Medal of Honor since this war received the medal posthumously.
4. In July, 1948, Army ROTC units were established at these two predominantly black schools.
5. He was the first black officer to be transferred to the regular Navy.
6. He is the first black officer to be promoted to four-star general in any branch of the U.S. armed forces.

7. Who was the highest ranking black American officer in France at the end of World War II?

8. Who was the leader of the famous 369th Infantry Band which played concerts in more than twenty-five cities in France (World War I) on a 2,000-mile tour?

9. He is the first black pilot to become a member of the famed U.S. Air Force prestigious precision flying group, the Thunderbirds.

10. Who was the first black astronaut trainee?

---

1. Major General Frederic E. Davidson 2. Phyliss Mae Dailey 3. Spanish-American War 4. Morgan State and Florida Southern 5. Ensign John W. Lee, on March 15, 1947 6. General Daniel "Chappie" James. In August, 1975, he assumed command of the North American Aerospace Defense Command 7. Lieutenant Colonel Otis B. Duncan of the 370th Infantry 8. Lieutenant James Reese Europe 9. Captain Lloyd Newton, of Ridgeland, South Carolina 10. Captain Edward J. Dwight, Jr.

MILITARY QUIZ 2

Match the following with the correct paragraph. There are twelve possible answers but only ten paragraphs. Some answers may be used more than once.

Dorie Miller	**Robert Humbles, Jr.**
Benjamin O. Davis, Sr.	**Benjamin O. Davis, Jr.**
George Roberts	**Wesley A. Brown**
Bernard W. Robinson	**Tuskegee Army Air Field**
Jesse Leroy Brown	**Hugh Mulzac**
99th Pursuit Squadron, in World War II	**Richard Nelson**

1. He was the first black Air Force general in the U.S. He was also the first black Air Force officer to command an air base.
2. It was the name of the first black unit in the Air Force.
3. On March 7, 1941, the first class of black pilots graduated from the segregated aviation school at this airfield.
4. He was the first black man accepted for pilot training in the U.S. Army Air Corps (1942).
5. He was the first black to win a commission in the U.S. Navy.
6. He was the first American hero of the Second World War.
7. He was the first black U.S. merchant ship captain.
8. He was the first black general in the history of the U.S. armed forces. He was commanding officer of Harlem's famed 369th Coast Artillery Regiment prior to becoming a general.
9. In 1949, he became the first black to graduate from the U.S. Naval Academy.
10. On October 23, 1948, he became the first black to be commissioned and assigned to duty as an aviator by the U.S. Navy.

*1. **Benjamin O. Davis, Jr.** 2. **The 99th Pursuit Squadron**, in World War II 3. **Tuskegee Army Air Field** 4. **George Roberts.** He graduated with the first class from Tuskegee Army Air Field in 1942. He was the first black officer to command a racially mixed group 5. **Bernard W. Robinson**, a Harvard medical student, won a commission in the U.S. Naval Reserve in 1942 6. **Dorie Miller**, a messman. He manned a machine gun during the Japanese attack on the American fleet at Pearl Harbor, downed four enemy aircraft and was awarded the Navy Cross for valor in combat 7. **Hugh Mulzac** became captain of the Booker T. Washington in 1942 8. **Benjamin O. Davis, Sr.** 9. **Wesley A. Brown** 10. **Jesse Leroy Brown***

MILITARY QUIZ 3

Match the following with the correct paragraph. There are twelve possible answers but only ten paragraphs. Some answers may be used more than once.

Jesse Leroy Brown	**Nancy C. Leftenant**
October 30, 1952	**Richard E. Moore**
Edith De Voe	**October 30, 1954**
24th Infantry	**Samuel L. Gravely**
Wesley A. Brown	**William Thompson**
Edna Young	**82nd Infantry**

1. He was the first black naval officer killed in the Korean conflict. He was killed in a vain attempt to save the life of a squadron mate. He was awarded the Medal of Honor. The Navy named a destroyer escort after him in February of 1971.

2. On June 3, 1949, he became the first black commissioned officer in the United States Navy to graduate from the U.S. Naval Academy.

3. In July, 1950, a black unit recaptured the city of Yech'on, Korea, after a sixteen-hour battle, the first break in the steady withdrawal in the face of the North Korean advance. It was the first U.S. victory in Korea. The name of the unit was:

4. The Defense Department announced complete abolition of black units in the armed forces on this date.

5. On November 1, 1950, she became the first black WAVE in the regular Navy. She was among the first six females sworn in.

6. He was the first black naval officer to command a U.S. warship.

7. He was the first black to be commissioned a captain in the Illinois National Guard.

8. On June 21, 1951, this native of Brooklyn, New York, was awarded the Medal of Honor posthumously for heroism in Korea. This was the first grant of a Medal of Honor to a black since the Spanish-American War.

9. She was the first black in the regular Army nurse corps.

10. She was the first black nurse to be transferred to the regular Navy (January 6, 1948).

---

1. Jesse Leroy Brown 2. Wesley A. Brown 3. 24th Infantry Regiment 4. October 30, 1954 5. Edna Young 6. Lieutenant Commander Samuel L. Gravely assumed command of the destroyer escort USS Falgout on January 31, 1962. He has since been promoted to admiral 7. Richard E. Moore 8. William Thompson 9. First Lieutenant Nancy C. Leftenant, in 1948 10. Edith De Voe

---

Movies

The first movies that blacks appeared in were mockeries of black society and depicted black characters as childlike, happy-go-lucky and the socially and intellectually inferior servants of white society. Starting in 1902 and extending over a sixty-year period, blacks found great difficulty in attaining roles that were not stereotyped and dehumanizing. Prior to the late 1940s, the big movie houses seemed set on perpetuating a caste system in America that placed blacks at the lower level of the social structure.

It appears that 1948 was the beginning of a somewhat altered role for blacks in movies. Films regarding the problems of blacks in America began to appear on screens across the country. While not portraying blacks as heroes, many of these films are serious examinations of black-white relations. If you recall the films *The Jackie Robinson Story* and *Native Son,* you will probably remember that while they might have been entertaining, they were critiques of the American system of social justice, and so it was with many other films.

In recent years, there has been a transition in the movie industry. Blacks now play leading roles that portray them as something other than servants of the "masters." The industry has also opened its ranks to black producers, directors, writers, cameramen and others whose participation is critical in the production of a film.

MOVIES QUIZ 1

1. What was the first film directed by a black in modern times?

   a. ***The Learning Tree***
   b. ***Home of the Brave***
   c. ***Wattstax***
   d. ***Blacula***

2. What film is considered responsible for ushering in the black "superstud" vogue?

   a. ***Cotton Comes to Harlem***
   b. ***The Chicago Connection***
   c. ***Sweet Sweetback's Baadasssss Song***
   d. ***Shaft***

3. In what film did black composer Isaac Hayes win an Academy Award for best musical score?

   a. ***Come Back Charleston Blue***
   b. ***Shaft***
   c. ***Superfly***
   d. ***Sounder***

4. What was the first black horror film?

   a. *Blackenstein*
   b. *Blacula*
   c. *The Werewolf from Watts*
   d. *Slaughter*

5. What do the following blacks have in common? Rupert Crosse, James Earl Jones, Diana Ross, Cicely Tyson, Paul Winfield.

   a. They were all Academy Award nominees
   b. They were all in major Broadway productions before entering the movies
   c. They were all in their own TV series
   d. They were all Academy Award winners

6. What was the first film to use black actresses in key roles?

   a. *Los Boundries*
   b. *Darktown Jubilee*
   c. *Panama Hattie*
   d. *Imitation of Life*

7. What do the following blacks have in common? Hattie McDaniel, James Basket, Dorothy Dandridge, Sidney Poitier.

   a. They have each won an Academy Award
   b. They have each won an Emmy Award
   c. They have each won an Actors Alliance Award
   d. They are all members of the Actors Hall of Fame

8. What was the first motion picture to star a black man?

   a. *Darktown Strutter's Ball*
   b. *Darktown Jubilee*
   c. *Harlem Follies*
   d. *Harlem Capers*

9. What is the name of Sidney Poitier's first film?

   a. ***Lilies of the Field***
   b. ***Guess Who's Coming to Dinner***
   c. ***In the Heat of the Night***
   d. ***No Way Out***

10. Who directed the popular film *Shaft*?

   a. **Berry Gordy, Jr.**
   b. **Sam Lucas**
   c. **Richard Pryor**
   d. **Gordon Parks, Sr.**

---

1. The Learning Tree *(1969) featuring Kyle Johnson and directed by Gordon Parks, Sr.* 2. Sweet Sweetback's Baadasssss Song *(1971) featuring Melvin Van Peebles, produced by Melvin Van Peebles, and directed by Melvin Van Peebles* 3. Shaft 4. Blacula 5. *They were all Academy Award nominees* 6. Imitation of Life *(1934) featuring Louise Beavers and Fredi Washington* 7. *They have each won an Academy Award* 8. Darktown Jubilee *(1914) starring Bert Williams* 9. No Way Out *(1950)* 10. *Gordon Parks, Sr.*

MOVIES QUIZ 2

Read the description and identify the movie. There are twelve answers, but only ten descriptions. Some answers may be used more than once.

In the Heat of the Night
The Watermelon Man
Black Gun
A Raisin in the Sun
Trouble Man
A Patch of Blue
The Split
To Kill a Mockingbird
The Scalphunters
Ice Station Zebra
Guess Who's Coming to Dinner
To Sir with Love

1. This 1961 movie starred Sidney Poitier, Claudie McNeil and Diana Sands. It is a film based on Lorraine Hansberry's award-winning play about an urban black family.
2. In this film Brock Peters and Estelle Evans have prominent roles. The 1963 release is based on Harper Lee's best-selling novel of 1960. The story concerns the defense of a black on trial for allegedly raping a white girl.
3. This is a moving story about a blind girl befriended by a young black. It stars Sidney Poitier, Elizabeth Hartman, Shelley Winters, Ivan Dixon and Wallace Ford. It was a 1966 production.
4. In 1967, Director Norman Jewison presented a drama of racial hate and prejudice fictionally set in an ugly little Mississippi town. The stars are Rod Steiger and

Sidney Poitier, acting out well-realized characters. Quincy Jones composed the music and Ray Charles sang the title song.

5. In this 1967 release, director James Clavell paints a picture of a black teacher who takes a post in a tough London school and battles to reach rebellious youngsters. It starred Sidney Poitier.

6. This 1968 picture is a black power western involving a fur trapper with a captured runaway slave stalking a scalp-hunting gent to retrieve stolen furs. A black, trying to gain his freedom by outwitting whites, proves that white supremacy isn't omnipotent. Ossie Davis is cast along with Burt Lancaster.

7. Director Stanley Kramer draws on a top-level cast which includes Sidney Poitier, Spencer Tracy and Katharine Hepburn. This 1968 movie deals with the question of interracial love and the problems of mixed marriage. The cast also includes Beah Richards.

8. Director John Sturges put Jim Brown in this suspenseful cold war thriller about a U.S. nuclear war submarine on a secret mission to a polar region with an unknown saboteur aboard. It was a 1968 release.

9. Director Gordon Fleming starred Jim Brown (in 1968) as a tough criminal who decides on one last caper before retiring — robbing the Los Angeles Coliseum.

10. Director Melvin Van Peebles made his American film debut in this 1970 picture. He casts Godfrey Cambridge and Estelle Parsons in a film about a man who turns colored overnight. It is a story perched on the fine edge between comedy and tragedy.

1. **A Raisin in the Sun** *2.* **To Kill a Mockingbird** *3.* **A Patch of Blue** *4.* **In the Heat of the Night** *5.* **To Sir with Love** *6.* **The Scalphunters** *7.* **Guess Who's Coming to Dinner** *8.* **Ice Station Zebra** *9.* **The Split** *10.* **The Watermelon Man**

MOVIES QUIZ 3

Read the description and identify the movie. There are twelve answers, but only ten descriptions. Some answers may be used more than once.

Sounder	***The Soul of Nigger Charley***
Blacula	***The World's Greatest Athlete***
Thunder Road	***Amazing Grace***
Book of Numbers	***Black Gun***
Trouble Man	***Island in the Sun***
Uptown Saturday Night	***Slaughter***

1. During the post–Civil War period, legendary Williamson learns that an ex–Confederate colonel is catching black people to be used as slaves in a Mexican fort. Williamson's efforts to protect a settlement of ex-slaves and Quakers and break the slave trade market make for exciting action.

2. Raymond St. Jacques stars in this comedy-drama about a black numbers operation in Arkansas. St. Jacques is a perfect father figure as the shrewd numbers man who'll go to great lengths to protect his operation and its people. Freda Payne made her acting debut as a society girl who falls in love with a numbers operator.

3. A bomb kills the parents of ex–Green Beret Captain Jim Brown. He learns that the syndicate performed the murders. Rip Torn, the actual murderer of Brown's parents, arrives with mistress Stella Stevens and objects when the local boss orders Stevens to play up to Brown.

4. This story tells of a year in the life of a young black family in the deep South, a year during which the father is arrested for stealing in order to get meat for the table, and the son is left to do his father's work. Later the boy finds a friendly black schoolteacher who presents him with a truly adult problem — whether to abandon his family and raise himself by studying with the teacher or stay at home as the one strong pair of hands about.

5. Cab driver Bill Cosby and steelworker Sidney Poitier take a night off from their wives to visit an after-hours gambling club where they and other customers are held up by four stocking-hooded thieves. When Poitier later learns that a $50,000 winning lottery ticket was in his stolen wallet, he and Cosby decide to track down the holdup men. The movie climaxes with some harrowing experiences over the ticket.

6. Coach John Amos and his assistant Tim Conway leave Merrivale College and journey to Africa after a disastrous losing streak in all sports. They discover Jan-Michael Vincent, a youth with remarkable athletic ability. Vincent was the son of missionaries and is now the godson of witch doctor Roscoe Lee Brown. Through trickery, Vincent is brought back to campus by Amos and Conway and coached to be a star in every sport. Vincent manages to salvage the honor of Merrivale College.

7. Moms Mabley meets Slappy White on his last day as a Pullman porter after 30 years on the job. Moms takes in the outgoing White, who had always wanted to be a song and dance man. Living next to Moms is Moses Gunn, a cultured politician running for mayor. Adviser Jim Karen promises that, if Gunn delivers the vote to the corrupt mayor, Dolph Sweet, he'll receive a $10 million urban renewal program in return. When Moms and Slappy learn about the plot, they decide that Gunn is being used as a pawn and persuade him to run an honest campaign and win on his own.

8. This movie features the volatile Jim Brown as a posh nightclub owner who is drawn into a confrontation with the "mob" when his younger brother is murdered by them. Brown moves into revengeful action and in an explosive, violent climax, Brown, Bernie Casey and others shoot it out with Landau's gang.

9. In 1780 Transylvania, an African prince asks Count Dracula to help in ending the slave trade. Dracula curses the prince to a life of vampirism. In 1972, the two decorators unwittingly turn loose the prince who kills both of them, setting off an epidemic of modern-day vampires.

10. Robert Hooks stars as Mr. "T" in a bullet-fast action-adventure drama. Mr. "T" settles anything or anyone for a price, usually a big one, and mostly using his own methods outside the law. Paula Kelly stars as Hook's loyal one-man girlfriend.

1. The Soul of Nigger Charley *2.* Book of Numbers *3.* Slaughter *4.* Sounder *5.* Uptown Saturday Night *6.* The World's Greatest Athlete *7.* Amazing Grace *8.* Black Gun *9.* Blacula *10.* Trouble Man

Organizations

The institutions of man have been used to perpetuate, to eliminate, to expand and to improve many aspects of American life. E. Franklin Frazier talked about the relationship of the black church and family to the well-being of black society during some of the most demeaning and oppressive years of the American experience.

The different organizations that are found within the realm of our varied institutional settings have worked diligently to foster an attitude of brotherhood and sisterhood and self-help among black men and black women. The purposes of these organizations include but are not limited to spiritual enlightenment, social improvement and economic development.

ORGANIZATIONS QUIZ 1

Match the following with the correct paragraph. There are twelve possible answers but only ten paragraphs. Some answers may be used more than once.

Robert W. Clayton
Liberia
James L. Farmer
Nigeria
New York City
Malcolm X (Little)
W. D. Fard
W. E. B. Du Bois
Washington, D.C.
The National Baptist Convention, U.S.A., Incorporated
Dr. Carter G. Woodson
NAACP

1. The Nation of Islam (better known as the Black Muslims) was founded in the 1930s by this man.
2. The first black YMCA was organized in this city by Anthony Bowen, a black man. It provided such programs as physical fitness, mental training, religious ideas, fellowship and vocational guidance.
3. He was the first director of CORE (Congress of Racial Equality). He was born in Marshall, Texas, and attended Wiley College and Howard University. He was a cofounder of CORE.
4. He was the first black president of the YMCA (elected on January 29, 1967).

5. The first Pan-African Congress met at the Grand Hotel in Paris, France, on February 19, 1919. The delegates included sixteen American blacks, twenty West Indians and twelve Africans. It was organized by this scholar.
6. This is the largest black organization in the United States. It has over 6,000,000 members.
7. He (1875–1950) founded the Association for the Study of Negro Life and History in 1915. He was the publisher of the *Journal of Negro History* and author of many books on the black man.
8. He (1925–1965) was a leader of the Black Muslims and founder of the Organization for Afro-American Unity. He was assassinated in 1965.
9. The first black sorority (Alpha Kappa Alpha) was organized in this city on January 15, 1908.
10. In 1817, the American Colonization Society was formed to settle freed blacks in what is now this country.

---

1. W. D. Fard. He was succeeded by Elijah (Poole) Muhammad 2. Washington, D.C. 3. James L. Farmer 4. Robert W. Clayton 5. W. E. B. Du Bois 6. The National Baptist Convention, U.S.A., Incorporated 7. Dr. Carter G. Woodson 8. Malcolm X (Little) 9. Washington, D.C. 10. Liberia

---

ORGANIZATIONS QUIZ 2

1. He (1887–1940) was a nationalist who organized the Universal Negro Improvement Association (UNIA), advocating a back-to-Africa movement for blacks in 1918 in New York City.

a. **Marcus A. Garvey**
b. **Andress E. Taylor**
c. **Thomas W. Black**
d. **Harold L. Aubery**

2. He is the executive secretary of the NAACP and former editor of *Crisis* magazine.

   a. **William Hutt**
   b. **Ulysses Davis**
   c. **Roy Wilkins**
   d. **Joseph Taylor**

3. He was the organizer and founder of the Opportunities Industrializations Centers of America, Inc. He is also a member of the Board of Directors of General Motors Corporation.

   a. **Dudley J. McDonald**
   b. **Edward B. Williams**
   c. **Leon H. Sullivan**
   d. **James C. Coleman**

4. She was the founder and first president of the National Council of Negro Women.

   a. **Sylvia Joyce Porter**
   b. **Margaret Hanson Miller**
   c. **Mary McLeod Bethune**
   d. **Aretha Ellen Johnson**

5. This organization was founded in January 1957 by sixty black leaders, most of them ministers from ten southern states. Dr. Martin Luther King, Jr., was its first president.

   a. **Committee on Freedom (COF)**
   b. **Southern Christian Leadership Conference (SCLC)**
   c. **National Black Ministers (NBM)**
   d. **National Brotherhood Committee (NBC)**

6. The purpose of this organization was to demonstrate black economic and political power by applying pressure to white businesses in an effort to acquire more jobs for blacks and by encouraging blacks to own and operate their own businesses.

   a. **Black Economic Caucus**
   b. **Operation Survival**
   c. **Operation Breadbasket**
   d. **Black Business Bureau**

7. The leaders of this organization, who recently opened their doors to whites, teach their followers to "do for self" socially and economically.

   a. **the Nation of Islam**
   b. **the National Black Alliance**
   c. **Nation of Alliance**
   d. **Nation of True Believers**

8. When was the Congressional Black Caucus founded?

   a. **January, 1968**
   b. **January, 1969**
   c. **February, 1968**
   d. **February, 1969**

9. What is the motto of the Congressional Black Caucus?

   a. **Forge ahead, consider all, remember our roots**
   b. **We have no permanent friends, no permanent enemies, just permanent interests**
   c. **Consideration, moderation, integration**
   d. **Friendship is essential to the soul**

10. Who was the founder of the black Masons?

   a. **Elijah Poole**
   b. **Prince Hall**
   c. **Monroe Wilson**
   d. **Richard Allen**

1. Marcus A. Garvey   2. Roy Wilkins   3. Leon H. Sullivan   4. Mary McLeod Bethune   5. Southern Christian Leadership Conference (SCLC)   6. Operation Breadbasket   7. the Nation of Islam   8. January, 1969   9. We have no permanent friends, no permanent enemies, just permanent interests   10. Prince Hall, in Boston in 1787

Pioneers in Business

The black man in America has made many contributions to the national economy and the black community through his business enterprises. There are few areas, if any, that have not been explored as a means of improving the economic status of blacks by blacks.

Madame C. J. Walker became famous and rich in the cosmetic industry. The insurance industry contributed greatly to the establishment of a black middle class, as did several other businesses.

As black businesses were established, the need to fight racism in the business sector was apparent. Therefore, the National Black Business League was organized to assist in the development and perpetuation of worthwhile business ventures. To the same end, the Minority Business Enterprise was created.

Today, there are many examples of successful black businesses in the United States. They range from A to Z in scope and are supporters of the national economy.

PIONEERS IN BUSINESS QUIZ

1. When and where was the first black owned and operated bank chartered?

   a. **March 2, 1888, in Richmond, Virginia**
   b. **August 16, 1922, in Forest City, Arkansas**
   c. **May 14, 1936, in Jackson, Mississippi**
   d. **September 12, 1926, in Cottonplant, Arkansas**

2. Who was the first black man to become a director of a U.S. automobile company?

   a. **Harry S. Taylor**
   b. **Leon H. Sullivan**
   c. **Levi Jackson**
   d. **Rev. Rember Burthey**

3. Who was the first black gold miner in California?

   a. **Nathaniel Fairfax**
   b. **Clavin Fields**
   c. **Kinnard Jones**
   d. **Waller Jackson**

4. What is the largest *privately held* black business in the U.S.?

   a. **Atlanta Life Insurance Company**
   b. **Fuller Products**
   c. **Conyers Ford Agency**
   d. **Afro-Sheen Products**

5. What is the largest black insurance company in the world?

   a. **Supreme Liberty and Life Insurance Company**
   b. **Arkansas Mutual Insurance Company**
   c. **The North Carolina Mutual Life Insurance Company**
   d. **Golden State Mutual Insurance Company**

6. In what year was the National Negro Bankers Association founded?

   a. **1918**
   b. **1924**
   c. **1921**
   d. **1917**

7. In 1900, the National Black Business League was organized in the city of:

   a. **Philadelphia**
   b. **Detroit**
   c. **Boston**
   d. **Chicago**

8. In 1847 the taxable income of free blacks in Philadelphia was estimated at:

   a. **$200,000**
   b. **$300,000**
   c. **$400,000**
   d. **$600,000**

9. Clothing stores in black neighborhoods:

   a. **are less likely to offer credit**
   b. **are more likely to have huge mark-ups**
   c. **often use courts to assist in collections**
   d. **all of the above**

10. Retail mark-up in black neighborhoods tends to be higher in:

   a. **work-related items**
   b. **recreational items**
   c. **recreational household items**
   d. **functional items**

---

1. March 2, 1888, in Richmond, Virginia 2. Leon H. Sullivan was elected to the Board of Governors of the General Motors Corporation in January, 1971 3. Waller Jackson, who sailed around Cape Horn from Boston in 1849. Several hundred other black miners followed 4. Atlanta Life Insurance Company 5. The North Carolina Mutual Life Insurance Company 6. 1924 7. Boston 8. $400,000 9. All of the above 10. Functional items, such as sewing machines, washing machines, dryers, etc.

Publishing

The power inherent in the press and other instruments of the mass media is uncanny. Some claim that a free press is an indicator of a stable society, for no man is free until the press itself is free. Through the communication industry, the citizenry is informed of events directly affecting every aspect of their lives. To be uninformed is to have limited options. One can hardly participate fully in decision-making processes when one's level of awareness is low.

Blacks have used the printed word to protest anti–civil rights activities, including lynchings, segregation in public places, inadequate jobs and other forms of racism. On the other hand, the press has, in some cases, sought to illustrate the good that people are capable of doing in all areas of human life.

Radio, movies and television are important information-gathering and entertainment instruments. There are not many homes in the United States today that do not have a radio and/or television set. As you listen to the radio and watch the television and movies in theaters, you often engage in these activities because of the contributions made to the industry by blacks.

PUBLISHING QUIZ 1

1. What black magazine has the highest-paid monthly circulation of any black publication in history?

   a. *Ebony*
   b. *Jet*
   c. *Essence*
   d. *Black Scholar*

2. *The Liberator*, a newspaper that strongly advocated the abolition of slavery and the moral and intellectual elevation of blacks, was first published in Boston on:

   a. January 2, 1820
   b. January 2, 1831
   c. January 2, 1841
   d. January 2, 1861

3. Since the first black journalistic experiment in 1827, some 2,800 black newspapers have appeared in America. How many have survived till today?

   a. 246
   b. 153
   c. 119
   d. 103

4. What was the name of the first newspaper founded by a black man in America?

   a. ***The Underground Railroad***
   b. ***Freedom's Journal***
   c. ***Striding for Freedom***
   d. ***The Free Press***

5. Who was the founder of the Baltimore *Afro-American*?

   a. **Louis Graves**
   b. **Robert M. Blake**
   c. **Bernard Jefferson**
   d. **John H. Murphy**

6. Of the following black publications, which was started first?

   a. ***Jet***
   b. ***Ebony***
   c. ***Hue***
   d. ***Black World***

7. The first editor of *Crisis*, the official organ of the NAACP, was:

   a. **Walter White**
   b. **W. E. B. Du Bois**
   c. **A. Philip Randolph**
   d. **Roy Wilkins**

8. In what year did the first edition of *Crisis* appear?

   a. **November, 1910**
   b. **November, 1908**
   c. **November, 1912**
   d. **November, 1914**

9. Who was the founder of *Muhammad Speaks*, the Black Muslim newspaper?

   a. **Malcolm X**
   b. **Muhammad Ali**
   c. **Elijah Muhammad**
   d. **Lonnie Shabazz**

10. Who was the first black man to be selected as one of the ten outstanding young men of the year (1951) by the U.S. Junior Chamber of Commerce?

a. Carl Rowan
b. William Rasberry
c. John H. Johnson
d. Robert Goodpaster

---

1. Ebony 2. January 2, 1831 3. 153 4. Freedom's Journal 5. John H. Murphy 6. Black World, formerly Negro Digest 7. W. E. B. Du Bois 8. November, 1910 9. Malcolm X 10. John H. Johnson

---

PUBLISHING QUIZ 2

1. It was the first commercially successful black slick magazine in the U.S.

   a. *Sepia*
   b. *Negro Digest*
   c. *Crisis*
   d. *Freedom*

2. On December 3, 1847, he published his first issue of his abolitionist newspaper, *The North Star*. His name is:

   a. David Ruggles
   b. Raymond Williams
   c. Edward Washington
   d. Frederick Douglass

3. Born in 1925, he is a writer, journalist, former deputy assistant secretary of state, ambassador to Finland, U.N. alternate delegate and director of the U.S. Information Agency. He is:

   a. Carl T. Rowan
   b. Ofield M. Dukes
   c. Louis W. White
   d. Togo J. West

4. It was the first black city newspaper to serve the needs of the many migrants to the North.

   a. Chicago *Defender*
   b. Philadelphia *Eagle*
   c. Detroit *Courier*
   d. Pittsburgh *Courier*

5. It was the first black magazine in the U.S., published in New York by David Ruggles, a black abolitionist.

   a. **Boston *Gazette***
   b. **Chicago *Winds***
   c. ***Mirror of Freedom***
   d. ***Mirror of Liberty***

6. It was the most famous of all black abolitionist newspapers.

   a. ***Northern Light***
   b. ***North Trails***
   c. ***North Star***
   d. ***North Journeys***

7. Aside from his abolitionist activities, he is said to have been a great lecturer and newspaper editor. His name is:

   a. **Frederick Douglass**
   b. **Seaton Andrews**
   c. **Lyle Murphy**
   d. **Andrew Billingsley**

8. It was the former name of the magazine *Black World*.

   a. ***Negro Digest***
   b. ***Negro Progress***
   c. ***The Negro Spokesman***
   d. ***Negro Citizenship***

9. It is the city where the Johnson Publications are headquartered.

   a. **Memphis, Tennessee**
   b. **Detroit, Michigan**
   c. **St. Louis, Missouri**
   d. **Chicago, Illinois**

10. On January 20, 1918, she became the first black city editor of a New York newspaper, the New York *Age*.

    a. **Mary Finger**
    b. **Alice Lightfoot**
    c. **Mary Ludden**
    d. **Alice James**

---

1. Negro Digest 2. Frederick Douglass 3. Carl T. Rowan 4. Chicago Defender 5. Mirror of Liberty 6. North Star 7. Frederick Douglass 8. Negro Digest 9. Chicago, Illinois 10. Mary Finger

---

Religion

It has long been conceded that religion has been an important motivating force in the development of the black community. Historically and contemporaneously, no other social institution equals the church as the center of black communal life. As a result, the church and its concerns are held in high esteem in the black community. The church, in the early days of its development, became a place where *brothers and sisters* could get away from the problems of the world. Its purpose, aside from the primary goal of helping black people experience God's love, was (and still is) to comfort and to encourage the congregation to survive the deprivation of racism and not be destroyed by it.

During the days of slavery, many black ministers preached for the love of God as well as the abolition of slavery. From the pulpit, Henry H. Garnet called for slave rebellions and advocated the black man's return to Africa. Because they could not worship and be respected in white churches, several black men pulled away from the white churches they attended and founded their own where they could surely be treated with respect.

The church played an important role in the educational and economic and political aspects of the black community.

RELIGION QUIZ 1

1. Who was the first black Roman Catholic bishop in the U.S.?

   a. Gilbert A. Maddox
   b. James A. Healy
   c. William S. King
   d. Alonzo G. Smith

2. In 1794, the first black Episcopal congregation in the U.S. was founded in the city of:

   a. Detroit, Michigan
   b. Philadelphia, Pennsylvania
   c. Hartford, Connecticut
   d. Washington, D.C.

3. The first formal separate black Methodist denomination was started in 1813 in the city of:

   a. Greensboro, North Carolina
   b. Memphis, Tennessee
   c. Wilmington, Delaware
   d. Cleveland, Ohio

4. Who was the first black Roman Catholic priest in America?

   a. **Van Christoff**
   b. **Reginal Kilgore**
   c. **James A. Healy**
   d. **Carlton Vesey**

5. The first black YMCA was organized in this city on February 27, 1853.

   a. **Springfield, Massachusetts**
   b. **Newport, Rhode Island**
   c. **Boston, Massachusetts**
   d. **Washington, D.C.**

6. The first black rector in the U.S. was:

   a. **Absalom Jones**
   b. **Lovell Jones**
   c. **Lorenzo Smith**
   d. **Herbert Smith**

7. Who is known as the "Father of the Gospel Song"?

   a. **Dr. Alex Bradford**
   b. **Dr. Thomas A. Dorsey**
   c. **Dr. Joe E. Tex**
   d. **Dr. Rember Burthey**

8. Who was the founder of the African Methodist Episcopal Zion Church (AMEZ)?

   a. **James Banks**
   b. **James Baylor**
   c. **James Lightfoot**
   d. **James Varick**

9. The pre–Civil War minister who advocated black emigration to Africa was:

   a. **Henry H. Garnet**
   b. **Knox Strayhorne**
   c. **John H. Judkins**
   d. **Lewis E. White**

10. The Colored Methodist Episcopal Zion Church was established in the city of:

a. Chicago **c. Richmond**
b. New York **d. Louisville**

---

1. James A. Healy 2. Philadelphia, Pennsylvania 3. Wilmington, Delaware 4. James A. Healy 5. Washington, D.C. 6. Absalom Jones 7. Dr. Thomas A. Dorsey 8. James Varick 9. Henry H. Garnet 10. New York

---

RELIGION QUIZ 2

Read the possible answers and pick the correct ones based on the descriptions that follow.

1. **a. Theodore S. Wright** **c. Albert A. Banks**
b. Seldon W. Cheek **d. Cleophus N. Robinson**

He was the first black recipient of a theological degree in the U.S. (Princeton Seminary).

2. **a. Mark James** **c. Chester Smith**
b. Augustus Tolton **d. Brodus Butler**

On April 24, 1886, he became the first full-blooded black American ever to be ordained for the priesthood.

3. **a. Richard Crawford** **c. Richard Cole**
b. Richard Allen **d. Richard Freeman**

He was born a slave but purchased his freedom in 1777, the same year in which he was converted. He preached frequently at the St. George Methodist Church in Philadelphia where the officials planned to segregate the blacks who came to hear him. On one occasion he and William White were pulled from their knees during prayer because they were in a section reserved for whites. He then made a firm resolution to establish a church where blacks could worship as they pleased and not be subject to such indignities. The African Methodist Church grew from this determination.

4. **a. Virgil Jones** **c. Clarence Haynes**
 b. James Fuller **d. Lemuel Hanes**

He was the first black pastor of a white congregation. The church was in Torrington, Connecticut, in 1785.

5. **a. John Glouchester** **c. Fred Williams**
 b. Louis Graves **d. Donald Sherrard**

In 1812, he became the first black minister of a Presbyterian church.

6. **a. Melvin Webb** **c. William Jones**
 b. Absalom Jones **d. James Stapleton**

He was the first black rector in the U.S. He was also co-founder of the African Methodist Episcopal (AME) Church and was the leader of the exodus from Methodist churches after refusing to be seated in the church balcony reserved for blacks.

7. a. **Antoine Blanc** c. **Carter Collins**
   b. **Owsley Spiller** d. **James Lightfoot**

He organized the first black Catholic sisterhood in the U.S. in 1792.

8. a. **Charles King** c. **Reginal West**
   b. **George Hayes** d. **Thomas Kilgore**

He was the black minister and civil rights leader who was unanimously elected the first black president of the predominantly white American Baptist Convention in Boston, on May 17, 1969.

9. a. **Theodore King** c. **Sterling Cary**
   b. **Booker Wright** d. **Elijah Williams**

He was the first black to hold the office of president of the National Council of Churches. He was elected on December 7, 1972.

10. a. **Wardell H. Smith** c. **Sylvester A. Cornish**
    b. **Chester H. Smith** d. **Samuel E. Cornish**

He organized the first black Presbyterian church in the U.S. He was also editor of the first black newspaper in New York, entitled *Freedom's Journal.*

---

1. Theodore S. Wright 2. Augustus Tolton 3. Richard Allen 4. Lemuel Hanes 5. John Gloucester 6. Absalom Jones 7. Antoine Blanc 8. Thomas Kilgore 9. Sterling Cary 10. Samuel E. Cornish

---

RELIGION QUIZ 3

1. He was the founder of the first African Presbyterian church. Born in Kentucky in 1896, he had a rich musical voice and led a full life. Four of his sons became Presbyterian ministers.

   a. **John Glouchester**
   b. **Lester Maddox**
   c. **Albert A. Banks**
   d. **Fletcher B. Routt**

2. He was largely responsible for organizing the Abyssinian Baptist Church in New York.

   a. **Jonathan H. Rodgers**
   b. **Clarence E. Anderson**
   c. **William L. Powell**
   d. **Thomas Paul**

3. He was the first black minister to be awarded the Nobel Peace Prize.

   a. **Martin Luther King, Jr.**
   b. **Coleman J. Young**
   c. **Albert Cleage, Jr.**
   d. **Henry Eiland**

4. In 1838, he became the first black pastor of the AME Zion Church in Boston, Massachusetts.

   a. **Jehial C. Beman**
   b. **Edward H. Frankland**
   c. **Lester B. Granger**
   d. **Willie S. Lightner**

5. In 1836, these noted churchmen founded the first black Baptist Church in Baltimore, Maryland.

   a. **M. C. Clayton and Noah Davis**
   b. **C. J. Franklin and S. S. Lightfoot**
   c. **L. W. Freeman and S. M. Loughton**
   d. **J. E. Edwards and W. W. Layton**

6. On October 20, 1870, two men organized the CME Church. They were:

   a. **Bishops Vanderhorst and Baylor**
   b. **Bishops Vanderhorst and Kilby**
   c. **Bishops Miles and Vanderhorst**
   d. **Bishops Miles and Kilby**

7. In what year was the National Baptist Convention organized?

   a. **1885**
   b. **1895**
   c. **1890**
   d. **1899**

8. In 1816, the African Methodist Episcopal Church was founded in the city of:

   a. **Dayton, Ohio**
   b. **Philadelphia, Pennsylvania**
   c. **Chicago, Illinois**
   d. **Baltimore, Maryland**

9. Who was the founder of Black Christian Nationalism?

   a. **Virgil Lee Jones**
   b. **Albert Cleage, Jr.**
   c. **William L. Jones**
   d. **Albert A. Banks**

10. What was the first social institution controlled entirely by blacks that gave them an opportunity to develop leadership qualities and be offered relief and hope prior to and after the Reconstruction years?

a. the schools **c. the church**
b. the plantations **d. the Masonic Order**

---

1. John Gloucester 2. Thomas Paul 3. Martin Luther King, Jr. 4. Jehial C. Beman 5. M. C. Clayton and Noah Davis 6. Bishops Miles and Vanderhorst 7. 1895 8. Philadelphia, Pennsylvania 9. Rev. Albert Cleage, Jr. 10. the church

---

Slavery

Many black historians have dealt with the question of slavery and on the manner in which people viewed it. A recent attempt at setting the record straight has been advanced by John W. Blassingame in his book *The Slave Community.* Blassingame asserts that the view of slave life was distorted by those who were in power during this shameful period of American history. In his preface, he wrote that the "clearest portrait the planter has drawn of the slave is the stereotype of Sambo, a submissive half-man, half-child." Those who are students of Afro-American history may find several accounts to the contrary; however, those who are casual observers of American history may never have the opportunity to read about or discuss the community in which slaves lived.

In this section, the subtopic relative to slavery that receives the most attention is the quest for freedom. While the word freedom lends itself to many philosophical interpretations, it is generally agreed that freedom means living with an absence of obligations to an oppressive situation. The oppressive situation that we are concerned with is slavery. No individual can stride progressively toward his goal of freedom and in truth be like the "Sambo stereotype."

SLAVERY QUIZ 1

1. Emancipation Proclamation Day is on this day.

   a. January 1 **c. October 1**
   b. February 1 **d. November 1**

2. During August 21–22, 1831, he led a slave revolt in Southhampton County, Virginia. Some sixty whites were killed. He was not captured until October 30, 1831.

   a. Denmark Vesey **c. Dred Scott**
   b. Nat Turner **d. Matthew Robinson**

3. She (1820–1913) was born a slave and escaped to freedom. Known as the "Moses" of blacks, she was most famous as one of the conductors of the Underground Railroad. She returned to the South on nineteen different occasions to guide more than 300 slaves to their freedom.

   a. Rebecca Talbert **c. Helen Rankin**
   b. Ruth Black **d. Harriet Tubman**

4. In 1801, this state prohibited slave trade..

   a. New York **c. Connecticut**
   b. Michigan **d. Maryland**

5. During the period 1897 to 1938, four states enacted laws disenfranchising blacks and abridging their voting rights in response to the northern migration following enactment of southern manumission laws. The four states were New York, Pennsylvania, New Jersey and:

   a. Delaware **c. Connecticut**
   b. Maine **d. New Hampshire**

6. He (1800–1858) was the most famous slave of his time. In "free" territory he brought suit for his freedom. The Supreme Court ruled against him and thereby denied blacks the right of citizenship. His name is:

   a. Scott Joplin **c. Walter Dunkin**
   b. Hugh Scott **d. Dred Scott**

7. The son of a Mendi chief, he was seized by slavers in 1839. He was purchased in Havana, Cuba, and put on the ship *Armistad* with others for the trip to Principe. They seized the ship, killed the captain and ordered the owners to steer toward Africa. The U.S. Navy intercepted the ship and arrested him and his men. He was freed by the Supreme Court and returned to Sierra Leone in 1842. His name is:

   a. Joseph Cinque **c. Jefferson Abrams**
   b. Lester Lyles **d. Wilson Pickett**

8. The first abolitionist society in America was organized in Philadelphia. The president of this society was:

a. **Benjamin Franklin**
b. **John Adams**
c. **Andrew Longworth**
d. **George Blair**

9. He was one of the first men of African blood to escape slavery. He helped more than 600 slaves to escape from the southern states. He published the quarterly magazine *Mirror of Liberty* in 1838. This was the first magazine to be edited by a black American.

a. **Lester B. Granger**
b. **Clyde Holbrook**
c. **Noles Carraway**
d. **David Ruggles**

10. In 1862, he became the acting Governor of Louisiana upon the impeachment of the incumbent.

a. **P. B. S. Pinchback**
b. **J. W. E. Pinchback**
c. **H. E. W. Pinchback**
d. **P. B. F. Pinchback**

---

1. January 1 2. Nat Turner 3. Harriet Tubman 4. New York 5. Connecticut 6. Dred Scott 7. Joseph Cinque 8. Benjamin Franklin 9. David Ruggles 10. P. B. S. Pinchback

---

SLAVERY QUIZ 2

1. True/False The Denmark Vesey conspiracy, one of the most elaborate slave-uprising plots on record, was betrayed on May 30, 1832. Vesey and thirty-six of his collaborators were hanged, while an additional 130 blacks and four whites were arrested.

2. True/False Frederick Douglass, abolitionist and statesman, was born in Tuckahoe, Maryland.

3. True/False Slaves sought legal means to obtain their freedom before the Emancipation Proclamation.

4. True/False The importation of slaves into America was banned in 1807. There had been too many examples of how slaves threatened the security of their "masters" by revolting.

5. True/False The first organized attack on the institution of slavery in British America was on February 18, 1688.

6. True/False Blacks were the only slaves in American history.

7. True/False On October 16, 1859, John Brown and his band of thirteen whites and five blacks attacked Harpers Ferry. Two of the blacks were killed, two were captured, and one escaped. Brown was hanged at Charleston, Virginia, on December 2, 1859.

8. True/False On August 30, 1800, Gabriel Prosser and Jack Bowler led eleven hundred fellow slaves in an attack on Richmond, Virginia. They were executed along with others after betrayal of the plot.

9. True/False In 1793, the Fugitive Slave Act was passed. It made it a criminal offense to harbor a slave or prevent his arrest.

10. True/False Black history in "English America" began on August 20, 1816, with the arrival of twenty blacks aboard a Dutch vessel.

1. True 2. True 3. True 4. True 5. True 6. False. Indians as well as some whites were placed into slavery 7. False. He was hanged at Charleston, West Virginia 8. True 9. True 10. False. It was 1619

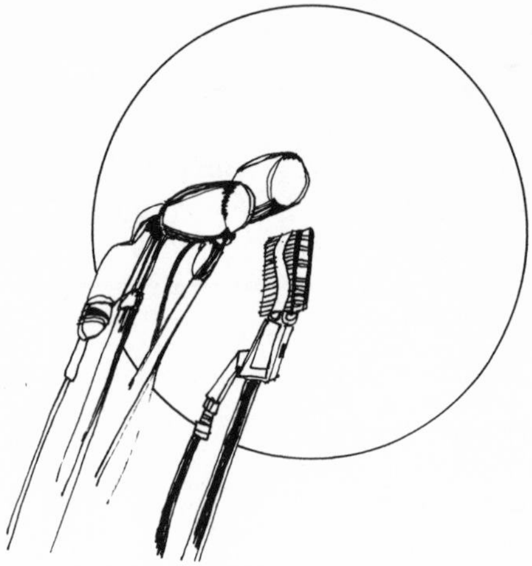

Identify the Person

Man's knowledge of the world around him is directly correlated with his knowledge of himself. For as his knowledge of himself increases, so does his knowledge of the world and how he fits into the social order of things. To understand himself, the black man must have an understanding of his ancestral background. This knowledge would help provide answers to the question, "Who and what am I?" Many attempt to answer this question solely by looking inward to analyze themselves rather than combining the internal search with an external search that would include an investigation of their ancestors. The suggestion here is that those who have difficulty understanding themselves should seriously consider a survey of history's great black personalities.

One such notable survey was accomplished by the late Mr. J. A. Rogers, an anthropologist and historian, who wrote a book entitled *World's Great Men of Color*. This book appears in two volumes. The first deals with Africa and Asia and historical figures before Christ. The second volume discusses blacks in Europe, South and Central America, the West Indies and the United States.

The influence of blacks on the American culture is no longer speculative. There have been many books on the subject and fresh analysis and interpretation is provided with each writing. A few notable blacks are discussed in this section.

IDENTIFY THE PERSON QUIZ 1

The following black persons were born outside of the United States. In what country were they born?

Names

1. Robert Bannister
   (Painter)
2. Stokely Carmichael
   (Civil Rights Leader)
3. Aime Cesaire
   (Writer)
4. Jean Brierre
   (Poet)
5. Kenneth B. Clark
   (Psychologist)
6. Jean Baptiste Point
   du Sable
   (Explorer)
7. Elijah McCoy
   (Inventor)
8. Marcus Garvey
   (Nationalist)
9. Richard B. Harrison
   (Actor)
10. Jan E. Matzeliger
    (Inventor)

Scrambled Clues

Haiti
Canada
Dutch Guiana
Trinidad
Martinique
Panama
Haiti
Canada
Jamaica
Canada

---

1. Canada 2. Trinidad 3. Martinique 4. Panama 5. Haiti
6. Haiti 7. Canada 8. Jamaica 9. Canada 10. Dutch Guiana

IDENTIFY THE PERSON QUIZ 2

The following black persons were born outside of the United States. In what country were they born?

Names	Scrambled Clues
1. Claude McKay (Poet)	Bahama Islands
2. Walter Adolphe Roberts (Writer)	Senegal
3. John Brown Russwurm (Educator)	Canada
4. Elliott Percival Skinner (Diplomat)	Virgin Islands
5. Andre Watts (Concert Pianist)	Brazil
6. Bert Williams (Vaudeville Star)	Jamaica
7. Phillis Wheatley (Poet)	Trinidad
8. Oscar Peterson (Pianist)	Jamaica
9. Roy Innis (Civil Rights Leader)	Germany
10. Bola Sete (Guitarist)	Jamaica

---

1. Jamaica 2. Jamaica 3. Jamaica 4. Trinidad 5. Germany 6. Bahama Islands 7. Senegal 8. Canada 9. Virgin Islands 10. Brazil

---

IDENTIFY THE PERSON QUIZ 3

Read the possible answers and pick the correct ones based on the *descriptions* that follow.

1. **a. James P. Blake**
   b. Robert C. Weaver
   c. Whitney M. Young, Jr.
   d. Ralph D. Abernathy

   He was a social reformer born in Lincoln Ridge, Kentucky. A writer on the problems of blacks, he was known for his syndicated newspaper column and his book *To Be Equal* (1964). He was director of the National Urban League, an organization of black citizens with some white participation whose purpose is to improve local living conditions and employment opportunities.

2. **a. Roland Jarvis Hayes**
   b. Andress Christopher Taylor
   c. Hobart Matthew Taylor
   d. Paul Laurence Dunbar

   He was a black poet, born in Dayton, Ohio. After being graduated from the Dayton High School in 1891, he worked as an elevator operator, a mechanic and a journalist. In 1897, he was employed on the staff of the Congressional Library, resigning in 1898 to give his attention entirely to his literary work.

3. **a. James Baldwin**
   b. Charles Kinnard
   c. Jesse Jackson
   d. David Blake

He is a novelist who was born in New York City and grew up in Harlem. He attended the DeWitt Clinton High School, where he edited a school magazine. He became a news reporter and soon afterward an essayist and novelist. His writings include *Go Tell It on the Mountain, Another Country* and *The Fire Next Time.* His writings criticize anti-black attitudes.

4. **a. Edmonia Davidson** **c. Mildred Alice Philips**
   b. Gloria Jackson **d. Mary McLeod Bethune**

   She was an American black educator born in Mayesville, South Carolina. After she was graduated from the Moody Bible Institute in 1895, she became a teacher, and in 1904 founded the Daytona (Florida) Normal and Industrial School for Girls, which has since been renamed (partially after her).

5. **a. Ralph J. Bunche** **c. Ralph J. Miller**
   b. William H. Hastie **d. William H. Bourroughs**

   He was an American diplomat, political scientist, and educator born in Detroit, Michigan, the grandson of an American slave. His studies at the University of California and later at Harvard University were mainly in the field of political science, a subject which he taught for several years at Howard University. During World War II he was a coordinator of information for the U.S. government in Africa and the Near East. In 1946, he was "loaned" by the State Department to the United Nations. His most notable service for that organization was in taking over the task of mediator in Palestine and bringing about a peaceful settlement of the dispute between Israel and the Arabs. He was awarded the Nobel Peace Prize in 1950.

6. a. **John H. Johnson** c. **Medgar W. Evers**
   b. **Howard Thurman** d. **W. E. B. Du Bois**

He was an American black writer, born in Great Barrington, Massachusetts. Educated at Fisk, Harvard and Berlin universities, he was professor of economics at Atlanta University from 1896 to 1910. In the latter year he resigned to edit and direct *Crisis* and other publications for the advancement of black people. He returned to Atlanta as a professor of sociology, 1933–1944. Among his best known books are *The Suppression of the Slave Trade, The Philadelphia Negro, John Brown* and *Quest of the Silver Fleece.*

7. a. **John H. Jenkins** c. **Malachi Greene**
   b. **Medgar Wiley Evers** d. **Howard Festus Cameron**

He was an American civil rights leader who was born in Decatur, Mississippi, and studied at Alcorn Agricultural and Mechanical College. In 1954, he became state field secretary of the NAACP and held that position until his death. He encouraged blacks to vote and organized boycotts against firms that practiced discrimination. He organized many chapters of the NAACP throughout Mississippi before he was shot and killed in front of his home in Jackson in 1963.

8. a. **George H. Thomas** c. **William Henry Hastie**
   b. **Robert M. Blake** d. **Melvin Washington**

He is a black American jurist and was born in Knoxville, Tennessee. He was graduated from Amherst College in 1925 and from Harvard Law School in 1930. After engaging in the general practice of the law, he was, in 1933, made assistant solicitor of the Department of the Interior. In 1937, he was named district judge of the Virgin Islands, where he served two years. Returning to the United States, he was dean of the Howard University School of Law from 1939 to 1946. He was then appointed governor of the Virgin Islands, serving from 1946 to 1949. In 1949, he was appointed a judge on the U.S. Circuit Court of Appeals.

9. **a. Mahalia Jackson** **c. Clara Ward**
b. Judy Stapleton **d. Henretta Franzel**

She was a black American singer born and educated in New Orleans. Having shown remarkable talent at an early age, she became a concert singer and recording artist. She is known especially for renditions of spiritual (gospel) songs.

10. **a. George C. Wheeler** **c. Clarence A. Guest**
b. John H. Johnson **d. Wardell Lott**

He is a publisher who was born in Arkansas City, Arkansas. After graduation from the Du Sable High School in Chicago, he studied at the University of Chicago and Northwestern University. The founder and president of a publishing company, he publishes such highly successful magazines as *Ebony* and *Jet.*

---

1. Whitney M. Young, Jr. 2. Paul Laurence Dunbar 3. James Baldwin 4. Mary McLeod Bethune 5. Ralph J. Bunche 6. W. E. B. Du Bois 7. Medgar Wiley Evers 8. William Henry Hastie 9. Mahalia Jackson 10. John H. Johnson

---

IDENTIFY THE PERSON QUIZ 4

Read the possible answers and pick the correct ones based on the *descriptions* that follow.

1. **a. Aretha Franklin** **c. Diana Ross**
   b. Roberta Flack **d. Leslie Uggams**

   She failed to win a part in her high school musical play. She signed up for a vocal class at school and quit because she was afraid that she would not do well. She was a skinny little girl. Her childhood home was a third-floor walkup in Detroit's black ghetto. Her father was a laborer who worked himself up to foreman and was an active member in his local union. Singing was always a part of her life. On Sundays she sang hymns with the congregation at the Baptist church and then later as a member of the choir. She became part of a singing group called the Primettes. The Primettes later became the Supremes, and she was on her way to becoming a millionaire.

2. **a. Lena Horne**
   b. Tamara Dobson
   c. Cicely Tyson
   d. Florence Edwards

   She has a distinguished career on stage and in television. It was her remarkable portrayal of Rebecca in the film *Sounder* which elevated her to stardom and won her an Academy Award nomination as best actress in 1973. Beginning her acting career in the Vinnette Carroll production of *Dark of the Moon* at the Harlem YMCA, she won the Vernon Rice Award for her performance in *The Blacks* as well as *Moon on a Rainbow Shawl.*

3. **a. Myland Brown** **c. James DePreist**
b. Robert Noland **d. Oscar Peterson**

He was born in Philadelphia, Pennsylvania, and is the associate conductor of the National Symphony Orchestra (Washington, D.C.). He is one of the handful of blacks to hold such a position. A first-prize winner of the Mitropoulos International Conductory Competition, he was assistant conductor of the New York Philharmonic for a season, after which he appeared as guest conductor with such important European orchestras as those of Rotterdam, Stockholm, Brussels and Berlin.

4. **a. Andre Watts** **c. Theodore Bacon**
b. Scott Joplin **d. Alex Bradford**

"A keyboard athlete of undisputed superiority, he is now at the height of his muscular power and has, in addition, the right combination of looks, charm and hint of mystery to qualify as an ideal American hero." These lines which appeared in the *New York Times* refer to this concert pianist who, at the age of sixteen, became the first black instrumental soloist since the turn of the century to appear with the New York Philharmonic Orchestra.

5. **a. Aretha Franklin** **c. Shirley Bassey**
b. Gladys Knight **d. Diana Ross**

She made her professional debut when she was twelve years old. She sang a solo in the church where her father was pastor. She was paid a fee of fifteen dollars and she immediately went out and bought a pair of roller skates. She started out in the church's choir when she was only eight. It wasn't long afterward that she formed a gospel singing group with her older sister, Erma, and two other girls.

6. a. **Fats Waller** c. **James P. Johnson**
   b. **C. C. Rider** d. **Scott Joplin**

His works published between 1895 and 1917 include fifty-three pieces for piano, ten songs and the opera *Treemonisha,* and three subsequently published, revised excerpts from *Treemonisha.* In all, twenty-one publishers are known to have brought out his music during his lifetime. He was a master composer of classic ragtime, and was for far too long a classic example of forgotten genius. He was the central figure and prime creative spirit of ragtime, a composer from whom a large segment of twentieth-century American music derived its shape and spirit. The recent movie *The Sting* featured some of his compositions. Brahms, Debussy and Stravinsky all admired his genius.

7. a. **Madame C. J. Prentice**
   b. **Madame C. J. Lawton**
   c. **Madame C. J. Walker**
   d. **Madame C. J. Waller**

She (1868–1919) was a leading cosmetic manufacturer, a highly successful businesswoman and one of the first American women millionaires. She gave freely of her wealth to worthy educational and charitable institutions.

8. a. **Casey Mann** c. **Robert Felter**
   b. **Paul R. Williams** d. **Andrew Bryant**

He is generally known as one of the leading architects in America. A native of Los Angeles, he was attending the Polytechnic High School when he first expressed a desire to become an architect. His teachers thought they were being kind when they advised him to aspire to something else, as "Negroes had no future in architecture." Determined to pursue his dream, he continued to prepare himself for his career. He studied at the Beaux Arts Institute of Design, the Los Angeles School of Art and Design, and earned a degree from the University of Southern California.

9. **a. Robert Bennett** **c. Robert Bentley**
   b. Luther McCaskil **d. Charles Drew**

He (1904–1950) was not yet fifty years old, but already his contribution to medicine had saved hundreds of thousands of lives during World War II. He was a pioneer in blood plasma preservation. Before his time there was no efficient way to store large quantities of blood plasma for use during emergencies or for use in wartime where thousands of lives depended on the availability of blood for blood transfusions. After him, this was no longer a problem, for he discovered ways and means of preserving blood plasma in what are commonly known as blood banks.

10. **a. Virgil L. Jones** **c. Prince Hall**
    b. Owsley G. Spiller **d. James L. Lightfoot**

He (1735–1807) was the founder of the first black Masonic lodge. He was born the son of an English father and a free black woman in Barbados in the British West Indies. At the age of twelve, he was apprenticed to a leather merchant. After a few years, he gave up his apprenticeship and, after working at a variety of jobs, finally came to Boston in 1765. Working in and around Boston, he saved enough money to buy property and to become a voter. During his spare time he educated himself.

1. Diana Ross 2. Cicely Tyson 3. James DePreist 4. Andre Watts 5. Aretha Franklin 6. Scott Joplin 7. Madame C. J. Walker 8. Paul R. Williams 9. Charles Drew 10. Prince Hall

IDENTIFY THE PERSON QUIZ 5

Read the possible answers and pick the correct ones based on the *descriptions* that follow.

1. **a. Malcolm X** **c. Carl 4X**
   b. Lonnie Shabazz **d. Jesse B. Blayton**

   He was an American black leader born in Omaha. He left school and later served a term in prison for burglary. Early in the 1950s he joined the Black Muslims and, in time, became chief lieutenant for Elijah Muhammad, their leader. He became disillusioned with the Black Muslims, and they suspended him in 1963. An eloquent and persuasive speaker, he founded the Organization of Afro-American Unity in 1964, urging black leadership of communities, cooperation with African nations and black conversion to Mohammedanism. He was shot to death as he addressed a rally in New York in 1965. His ideology has been adopted by many black leaders and his influence is widespread throughout black communities.

2. **a. Thurgood Freeman** **c. Thurgood Marshall**
   b. Carl Rowan **d. Carl Roister**

He is a lawyer, and was born in Baltimore, Maryland. He studied law at Howard University and in 1933 began practice in his native city. His work as counsel for the NAACP and the handling of civil rights litigation led to his appointment by President Kennedy as federal appellate judge in 1962 and President Johnson's appointment of him to the Supreme Court in 1967.

3. **a. Jesse Davis** **c. Owen Davis**
b. Lester Garrard **d. Jesse Owens**

Born in Alabama, he is a black American track and field star. Considered the greatest track athlete of the century, he first showed his exceptional skill while in high school in Cleveland, Ohio. In 1935, as a member of the Ohio State University track team, he broke three world records and tied a fourth in one day. At the Olympic games in 1936, he won four gold medals by equaling the world record in the 100-meter race (10.3 seconds), by breaking it in the 200-meter race (20.7) and also in the broad jump (26 feet $5\frac{5}{16}$ inches) and winning the 400-meter relay.

4. **a. Melvin Van Peebles** **c. Sidney Poitier**
b. Bert Williams **d. Lou Donaldson**

He is an actor who was born in Miami, Florida, and received part of his education in Nassau. After brief employment as messenger for a drugstore in Miami, he entered upon an acting career which has included award-winning roles in both stage and film plays. Some principal film parts were in *Cry, the Beloved Country*, *The Defiant Ones* and *Guess Who's Coming to Dinner*. He won the Academy Award for best actor in 1963 for his performance in *Lilies of the Fields*.

5. a. **Nichole Martin** c. **Willa Jasper**
   b. **Leontyne Price** d. **Pauline Grisby**

She is a singer, and was born in Laurel, Mississippi. She was educated at Central State College, Wilberforce, Ohio, and studied music at the Juilliard School in New York. Besides appearing as a soloist, she has sung in operas at Vienna, Berlin and elsewhere in Europe, and with the Metropolitan Opera Company in New York.

6. a. **Carl T. Rowan** c. **Leroi E. Dues**
   b. **Hugh J. Scott** d. **Leo G. Robinson**

He is a journalist, and was born at Ravenscroft, Tennessee. Specializing in mathematics at Oberlin College, he took a graduate degree in journalism at the University of Minnesota and began a distinguished reporting career with the Minneapolis *Tribune*. His coverage of news, including civil rights and events in Asia, has won him a number of awards. From 1961 to 1965, he served the State Department as ambassador to Finland.

7. a. **Jessica G. Turner** c. **Greta Jones**
   b. **Annie Wright** d. **Harriet Tubman**

She was a black abolitionist born in Dorchester County, Maryland. Born into slavery, she worked as a field hand until 1859, when she escaped to the North. Devoting herself to leading other slaves to freedom through the Underground Railroad, she is credited with helping more than 300 slaves gain freedom. Between trips, she worked as a cook and spoke at Boston anti-slavery meetings. During the Civil War, she worked with Union troops as a nurse and as a spy behind Confederate lines. After the war, she continued working for her people, setting up a home for needy blacks in Auburn, New York.

8. **a. Frederick Douglass** **c. Denmark Vesey**
b. Nat Turner **d. Howard Thurman**

He was an abolitionist born on the eastern shore of Maryland. As a slave, he worked on Maryland plantations, in Baltimore as a young house servant and in Baltimore shipyards as a caulker. He made a daring escape in 1838, and made his way to Massachusetts where he met Garrison and other abolitionists and became one of the foremost spokesmen of the abolitionist movement. He achieved prominence, and during his lifetime he served as United States secretary to Santo Domingo, as marshal and recorder of deeds for the District of Columbia and as United States minister to Haiti.

9. **a. Henrietta Hampton** **c. Marian Anderson**
b. Lillian Andrews **d. Constance Jackson**

In 1939, she was denied the use of Constitution Hall by the Daughters of the American Revolution. She sang on Easter Sunday before 75,000 people assembled at the Lincoln Memorial. She was the first black person to sing with the Metropolitan Opera Company (1941). Later she became a delegate to the United Nations. On January 7, 1955, she became the first black singer to be signed by the Metropolitan Opera Company for a leading role.

10. **a. Flip Wilson** **c. Richard Pryor**
b. Harland Randolph **d. Bill Cosby**

He began the race for success in show business at the age of nine, when he was given a small part in a school play about the famous nurse Clara Barton. At the last minute, the girl who was supposed to play Clara got sick and he was the only one who knew all the lines. So he got the part. He recalls, "I didn't decide right then and there to go into show business. I enjoyed making other kids laugh and it was also rather easy for me, but show business was not on my mind. I used my natural voice for Clara Barton. I didn't try to sound like a girl or anything. Just having that many lines was enough of a thrill for me because, until then, I was just going to be a wounded soldier in a play with nothing to do but groan."

---

1. Malcolm X 2. Thurgood Marshall 3. Jesse Owens 4. Sidney Poitier 5. Leontyne Price 6. Carl T. Rowan 7. Harriet Tubman 8. Frederick Douglass 9. Marian Anderson 10. Flip Wilson

---

IDENTIFY THE PERSON QUIZ 6

What are (or were) the following persons primarily known for?

Names	Scrambled Clues
1. Huey P. Newton	Musician
2. Walter E. Fauntroy	Chemist
3. William E. Brown, Jr.	Social Activist
4. Jimi Hendrix	Congressman
5. Barbara Jordan	Air Force General
6. Louis Stokes	Congresswoman
7. Edward Greer	Army General
8. Donny Hathaway	Singer
9. Ornette Coleman	Congressman
10. Percy L. Julian	Musician

1. Social Activist 2. Congressman 3. Air Force General 4. Musician 5. Congresswoman 6. Congressman 7. Army General 8. Singer 9. Musician 10. Chemist

IDENTIFY THE PERSON QUIZ 7

What are (or were) the following persons primarily known for?

Names	Scrambled Clues
1. James F. Hamlet	Army General
2. James L. Farmer	Publisher
3. John H. Johnson	Boxer
4. Arthur W. Mitchell	Theologian
5. Muhammad Ali	Actor-Playwright
6. Howard Thurman	Musician
7. Ossie Davis	Army General
8. Miles Davis	Army General
9. Harry W. Brooks, Jr.	Civil Rights Leader
10. Frederic Davison	Congressman

1. Army General 2. Civil Rights Leader 3. Publisher 4. Congressman 5. Boxer 6. Theologian 7. Actor-Playwright 8. Musician 9. Army General 10. Army General

IDENTIFY THE PERSON QUIZ 8

What are (or were) the following persons primarily known for?

Names	Scrambled Clues
1. Benjamin Brawley	Singer
2. Willie Mays	Track Star
3. John Conyers	Writer
4. Gwendolyn Brooks	Singer
5. Andre Watts	Historian
6. Kenneth B. Clark	Baseball Player
7. Della Reese	Congressman
8. James Baldwin	Poet
9. Rafer Johnson	Concert Pianist
10. Gladys Knight	Psychologist

---

1. Historian 2. Baseball Player 3. Congressman 4. Poet 5. Concert Pianist 6. Psychologist 7. Singer 8. Writer 9. Track Star 10. Singer

---

IDENTIFY THE PERSON QUIZ 9

What are (or were) the following persons primarily known for?

Names	**Scrambled Clues**
1. Shirley A. Chisholm	College President
2. Charles B. Rangel	Army General
3. Lena Horne	Congresswoman
4. John O. Killens	Congressman
5. Julius W. Becton, Jr.	Singer
6. Robert Hooks	Singer-Composer
7. James Cheek	Actor-Producer
8. George M. Shuffler, Jr.	Writer
9. Sterling Brown	Writer-Educator
10. Marvin Gaye	Army General

---

1. Congresswoman 2. Congressman 3. Singer 4. Writer 5. Army General 6. Actor-Producer 7. College President 8. Army General 9. Writer-Educator 10. Singer-Composer

---

IDENTIFY THE PERSON QUIZ 10

What are (or were) the following persons primarily known for?

Names	Scrambled Clues
1. Charles Wesley	Historian-Educator
2. William F. Russell	Basketball Star
3. Thurgood Marshall	Army General
4. Parren J. Mitchell	Operatic Singer
5. "Sugar" Ray Robinson	Army General
6. William L. Clay	Supreme Court Justice
7. Roscoe C. Cartwright	Boxer
8. Leontyne Price	College President
9. Roscoe Robinson, Jr.	Congressman
10. Cleveland Dennard	Congressman

---

1. Historian-Educator 2. Basketball Star 3. Supreme Court Justice 4. Congressman 5. Boxer 6. Congressman 7. Army General 8. Operatic Singer 9. Army General 10. College President

---

IDENTIFY THE PERSON QUIZ 11

What are (or were) the following persons primarily known for?

Names	**Scrambled Clues**
1. Johnny Mathis	Congressman
2. Anthony "Tony" Brown	College President
3. Thelonius Monk	Air Force General
4. Roscoe Robinson, Jr.	Army General
5. Lucius Theus	Singer
6. Thomas Clifford	Television Producer
7. Edward Brooke	Composer-Pianist
8. Wendell P. Russell	Air Force General
9. Ronald Dellums	Senator
10. Charles Diggs	Congressman

---

1. *Singer* **2.** *Television Producer* **3.** *Composer-Pianist* **4.** *Army General* **5.** *Air Force General* **6.** *Air Force General* **7.** *Senator* **8.** *College President* **9.** *Congressman* **10.** *Congressman*

IDENTIFY THE PERSON QUIZ 12

The following are excerpts from speeches made by some notable blacks. Identify the person who said:

1. Boxing is dying because too many blacks are fighting each other. This isn't a matter of racism. It's just that people like to root for their own side. It's human nature, not hatred. We Africans love Dick Tiger and Hogan Bassey. Nino Beneventui was great for the Italians. The English had Henry Cooper and Randy Turpin, who was black. They drew huge crowds when they fought against men of different countries or different skin. It's like a baseball team. You split up the greatest baseball team in the whole world and have them play each other and they won't draw nothing. But put them against somebody else and they will fill the stands. So what the white people need now is white fighters. They need an idol. They need a Jack Dempsey or a Gene Tunney.

   a. Muhammad Ali
   b. George Foreman
   c. "Sugar" Ray Robinson
   d. George Allen

2. It is an established, historical fact that when injustice and oppression exist, the people turn to the only recourse left — violence.

   a. Wendell P. Russell
   b. Adam Clayton Powell, Jr.
   c. Richard Hatcher
   d. Carl B. Stokes

3. The black people can't do it [influence the forthcoming national political conventions] alone. The women can't do it alone. The Chicanos can't do it alone. But together, the have-nots and the disillusioned can come together as delegates to tell those people who have been dominating these conventions for years: "Not this time, fellows."

   a. **Louise Wright**
   b. **Constance Jackson**
   c. **Shirley Chisholm**
   d. **Mary Stein**

4. No, I can't say blacks have no chance in America. We're free. We're doctors, lawyers, teachers and senators . . . look at me. I'm outspoken . . . I talk more than anybody. Nobody bothers me. There's opportunity . . . we can do anything. If somebody can't make it, it's his own fault.

   a. **Carl Gregory**
   b. **Muhammad Ali**
   c. **Owen Davis**
   d. **Leonard McKissik**

5. We [black people] are through believing. We are through hoping. We are through trusting the two major white American political parties. Hereafter, we shall rely on the power of our own black unity — if we form a third political movement, we shall take with us the Chicanos, Puerto Ricans, the Indians, the Orientals; and that is not all. We shall also take with us the best of white America.

   a. **Richard Hatcher**
   b. **Benjamin O. Davis, Jr.**
   c. **Carl Stokes**
   d. **Cleo G. Pruitt**

6. Integration is a good concept; but some people have pushed it purely as a way to help minority students. It is never sold on the right basis: To be able to function in a multiracial society is just as important for the white child as it is for a black child. [Regarding school busing for racial balance:] We're really not talking about a civil rights issue. We're talking about a quality education program with equal opportunity for all. That's the issue rather than just busing kids all over the place.

   a. **Michael Hall**
   b. **Wilson Riles**
   c. **Jessica Milligan**
   d. **Elnorah Hurd**

7. Without the option of a black political party, we [black people] are doomed to remain in the hip pocket of the Democratic Party and in the rumble seat of the Republican Party.

   a. **A. A. Banks**
   b. **Carlton Vesey**
   c. **Jesse L. Jackson**
   d. **Benjamin Henley**

8. The problems of the ghetto will have to be solved by the elite who come out of the ghetto. The real answers to the immense problems of our time will not be found by young people screaming in the streets, nor by "women libbers," or black people chanting slogans and calling names. Don't get me wrong. I am for Afro hairdos, for the study of black literature and art, for soul food, even if it has too much grease. [But] eating soul food will not solve a single problem of housing, employment or education.

   a. **Harland Carter**
   b. **Bennie Fitzgerald**
   c. **Beman Fitzhugh**
   d. **Bayard Rustin**

9. I think the American people are more disposed to be generous rather than just. I look over the country at the present time and I see Education Societies, Sanitary Commissions, Freedmen's Associations, and the like, all very good, but in regard to the colored people there is always more that is benevolent than just manifested toward us. What I ask for the Negro is not benevolence, not pity, not sympathy, but simply Justice.

a. Chester Himes
b. Walter White
c. Frederick Douglass
d. Seldon Walker

10. We may have all come over in different ships, but we're in the same boat now.

a. Whitney Young
b. James Nabritt
c. Rayford Logan
d. Samuel Nabritt

---

1. Muhammad Ali 2. Carl Stokes 3. Shirley Chisholm 4. Muhammad Ali 5. Richard Hatcher 6. Wilson Riles 7. Jesse L. Jackson 8. Bayard Rustin 9. Frederick Douglass 10. Whitney Young

---

Sports

It was Jesse Owens who won four gold medals in the 1936 Olympic games. Ralph Metcalfe participated in the 1932 and 1936 Olympic games. Black men at one time were the principal riders in the Kentucky Derby. In fact, Isaac Murphy was the first jockey to win three Kentucky Derbys. Joseph Louis Barrow, born in rural Alabama of impoverished parents, rose to international prominence as one of the greatest boxers to ever climb into a boxing ring. The list of great black athletes is too long to even begin to print it all in this book. Blacks may be found in practically every sport that is played in America. Their participation in sports was a vehicle through which they attained high economic and social standings.

As far as blacks were concerned, when most avenues of economic improvement were closed those gifted with athletic prowess were permitted to gain some measure of success by entertaining fans who came to see them either win or lose.

With their status achieved in sports, many athletes engaged in numerous activities designed to help their brothers and sisters who were less fortunate. Jesse Owens has been widely acclaimed for his support of youth programs. Joe Louis has helped raise money for charities. Ralph Metcalfe serves the nation as a representative to Congress from Chicago. "Brad" Holland, an All-American from Cornell University, became a leading educator as president of Hampton Institute. These have been no small accomplishments. If the past is any indication of what might occur in the future, many of America's great black athletes will continue to serve mankind in their own humanitarian ways.

BASEBALL QUIZ 1

Match the following with the correct paragraph. There are twelve possible answers but only ten paragraphs. Some answers may be used more than once.

Frank Robinson	**Moses Fleetwood Walker**
James ("Cool Papa") Bell	**Rube Foster**
Elston Howard	**John O'Neil**
Roberto Clemente	**Don Newcombe**
Henry ("Hank") Aaron	**Josh Gibson**
Willie Mays	**Bud Fowler**

1. He is the only baseball player to ever win the Most Valuable Player award in both major leagues. He was signed by the Cincinnati Reds after finishing high school in 1953. He was selected Rookie of the Year in 1956, the National League's Most Valuable Player in 1961 and Most Valuable Player in the American League in 1966.

2. He was the first black manager of a big league baseball team. He became playing-manager of the Cleveland Indians in 1974.

3. He was the first black major league baseball player in the U.S. He attended Oberlin College in Ohio, and then caught for the American Association's Toledo Club in 1884 when that league was ranked as a major.

4. He founded the National Negro Baseball League on February 13, 1920. The first teams were the Kansas City Monarchs, the Indianapolis ABCs, the Chicago American Giants, the Detroit Giants and a traveling team of Cuban Stars.

5. He was the first black baseball player to play on a white team. He starred at second base for the New Castle Club of Western Pennsylvania in the 1860s.

6. He was the first black coach of a major league baseball team. On May 30, 1962, he became the coach of the Chicago Cubs. Like so many black stars in baseball, he had learned to play in the Negro leagues. It was in the Negro American League that he got his start.

7. Born in 1931, he is an outstanding baseball player and is ranked among the finest home run hitters, base runners and defense outfielders in major league history.

8. He is known as the "home run champion" of all time. He was born in Mobile, Alabama, and began to play professional baseball with the Indianapolis Clowns of the Negro American League in 1952. The same year he was signed by the Milwaukee Braves of the National League. He broke Babe Ruth's record of home runs in 1974.

9. His spectacular career with the Pittsburgh Pirates began with the 1955 season. He was the recipient of the Golden Glove Award for fielding excellence and the Babe Ruth Award for his excellent plays in the World Series of 1971.

10. He regularly stole over a hundred bases each season. He was generally acknowledged as the fastest human ever to step onto a baseball diamond.

---

1. Frank Robinson 2. Frank Robinson 3. Moses Fleetwood Walker 4. Rube Foster 5. Bud Fowler 6. John O'Neil 7. Willie Mays 8. Henry ("Hank") Aaron 9. Roberto Clemente 10. James ("Cool Papa") Bell

---

BASEBALL QUIZ 2

1. Who was the first black major league baseball player in modern times?

   a. **Willie Mays**
   b. **Roy Campanella**
   c. **Jackie Robinson**
   d. **Satchel Paige**

2. Who was the first black baseball player ever to coach a big league ball club?

   a. **Elston Howard**
   b. **Roberto Clemente**
   c. **Maury Wills**
   d. **Larry Doby**

3. Who was the first black baseball player to play for the New York Yankees?

   a. **Satchel Paige**
   b. **Frank Peters**
   c. **Ernie Banks**
   d. **Elston Howard**

4. Who was the first black baseball player to be elected to the Baseball Hall of Fame?

   a. **Jackie Robinson**
   b. **Monte Irvin**
   c. **Josh Gibson**
   d. **Satchel Paige**

5. Who was the first black baseball player to be signed into the American League?

   a. **Jackie Robinson**
   b. **Larry Doby**
   c. **Rube Foster**
   d. **Henry ("Hank") Aaron**

6. Who was the first black baseball player to win the Cy Young Award as the most outstanding pitcher in the major leagues?

   a. **Don Newcombe**
   b. **Cleo Pruitt**
   c. **Maxzeller Thomas**
   d. **Charles Kinnard**

7. Sports writers generally agree that the greatest baseball pitcher who ever lived was:

a. **George Scales** c. **Oscar Johnson**
b. **Leroy "Satchel" Paige** d. **Box Makey**

8. What do the following black baseball stars have in common? Jackie Robinson, Roy Campanella, Satchel Paige, Josh Gibson, Buck Leonard, Monte Irvin, and Roberto Clemente.

a. **They have been elected to the Baseball Hall of Fame**
b. **They were American League stars**
c. **They were the highest-paid members of their teams**
d. **They were former basketball players**

9. He came to the Pittsburgh Pirates in 1955, scared, black and proud. When he died in that plane crash on New Year's Eve, 1972, he was still black and proud. His opponents were scared. His name is:

a. **Roberto Clemente** c. **Adolph Lugue**
b. **Ramon Herrera** d. **Rafael Almedia**

10. Who recently broke the home-run record of Babe Ruth?

a. **Frank Robinson** c. **Hank Aaron**
b. **Bob Gibson** d. **Willie Mays**

---

1. Jackie Robinson, who started big league playing on April 11, 1947 2. Elston Howard (a catcher) became a Yankee first base coach in 1969 3. Elston Howard, in 1955 4. Jackie Robinson, in 1961 5. Larry Doby, on January 31, 1948 6. Don Newcombe 7. Leroy "Satchel" Paige 8. They all have been elected to the Baseball Hall of Fame 9. Roberto Clemente 10. Hank Aaron

---

BASKETBALL QUIZ 1

1. In what city were the Harlem Globe Trotters founded?

   a. **New York, New York**
   b. **Chicago, Illinois**
   c. **Memphis, Tennessee**
   d. **Troy, New York**

2. What black basketball team was known as the premier professional team of its time?

   a. **Harlem Renaissance**
   b. **Los Angeles Sunsets**
   c. **Chicago Midlanders**
   d. **Washington Redskins**

3. Who was the first black American to coach a major sports team (the Boston Celtics)?

   a. **Bill Russell**
   b. **Sam Jones**
   c. **Stretch Caldwell**
   d. **John Estes**

4. Who was known as "Mr. Basketball" of his era?

   a. **Bill Russell**
   b. **Ronald Williams**
   c. **Mickey Gallimore**
   d. **Sweetwater Clifton**

5. Who was the first black athlete to sign a contract and become the first black player to play in the National Basketball Association?

   a. **Stretch Caldwell**
   b. **Leroy Dues**
   c. **Charles ("Chuck") Cooper**
   d. **Charles ("Chuck") Taylor**

6. Who was the first black basketball star to lead his league in scoring?

   a. **Chuck Cooper**
   b. **Wilt Chamberlain**
   c. **Bill Russell**
   d. **Sam Barnes**

7. Who was the first black basketball coach to be named Coach of the Year?

a. Ray Scott **c. Bill Russell**
b. Bob Antonine **d. James McLendon**

8. Who was the first black basketball coach to lead his team to an NBA title?

a. James F. Reynolds **c. Bill Russell**
b. Hook Jones **d. Sam Jones**

9. Who was the first black general manager in basketball?

a. Jimmy Collins **c. Hook Jones**
b. Chuck Cooper **d. Wayne Embry**

10. Who was the first black basketball player to lead his league in assists?

a. Jo Jo White **c. Oscar Robinson**
b. Don Barksdale **d. Sam Barnes**

1. Chicago, Illinois 2. Harlem Renaissance ("The Rens") 3. Bill Russell 4. Bill Russell 5. Charles ("Chuck") Cooper 6. Wilt Chamberlain, of the Philadelphia Warriors (37.6 ppp average), in 1959–60 7. Ray Scott, Detroit Pistons, 1973 8. Bill Russell, of the Boston Celtics, 1967–68 9. Wayne Embry, of the Milwaukee Bucks 10. Oscar Robinson of Cincinnati, with 690 during the 1960–61 season

BASKETBALL QUIZ 2

1. Who is the highest scorer in National Basketball Association history?

   a. **Wilt Chamberlain** c. **Jo Jo White**
   b. **Clyde Horton** d. **Bill Russell**

2. Who was the first black signed by the National Basketball Association?

   a. **"Big House" Gaines** c. **Jesse J. Mayes**
   b. **Chuck Cooper** d. **Jake Terrell**

3. Who is generally considered to be the greatest basketball dribbler of all times?

   a. **Don Barksdale** c. **Bob Douglass**
   b. **Marquis Haynes** d. **Goose Tatum**

4. The famous Harlem Magicians were organized on November 15, 1947, by:

   a. **Frank Williams** c. **Sad Sam Jones**
   b. **Marquis Haynes** d. **William Chrisp**

5. The first black to coach a major professional basketball team was:

   a. **Nathaniel Clifton** c. **James C. Hurd**
   b. **Earl Lloyd** d. **John McLendon**

6. In what year were the Harlem Globe Trotters founded?

   a. **1922**
   b. **1927**
   c. **1929**
   d. **1931**

7. In what year were the New York "Rens" founded?

a. 1923 **c. 1931**
b. 1929 **d. 1936**

8. Which black professional basketball team won the first world championship (1939)?

a. the Atlanta Flyers **c. the New York Renaissance**
b. the Detroit Techs **d. the Cleveland Challengers**

9. What was the name of the first outstanding black basketball team (1921)?

a. the Barnstormers of St. Louis
b. the Loendi Club of Western Pennsylvania
c. the Cosmos Club of Washington, D.C.
d. the Sunsets of Los Angeles

10. In what year was professional basketball integrated?

a. 1945 **c. 1955**
b. 1950 **d. 1960**

---

1. Wilt Chamberlain 2. Chuck Cooper, of Duquesne University 3. Marquis Haynes 4. Marquis Haynes 5. John McLendon, a former coach at Tennessee State University, began coaching the Denver Rockets in May, 1969 6. 1927, by Abe Saperstein 7. 1923 8. the New York Renaissance 9. the Loendi Club of Western Pennsylvania 10. 1950

BOXING QUIZ 1

1. Who was the first black professional to earn a living as a boxer?

   a. **Joe Louis**
   b. **Bill Richmond**
   c. **Henry Armstrong**
   d. **Jack Johnson**

2. According to most sports writers in the country, "pound for pound" the greatest all-round fighter that this country has produced (whole career considered) is:

   a. **Sugar Ray Robinson**
   b. **Ezzard Charles**
   c. **Tiger Flowers**
   d. **Floyd Patterson**

3. The first black to win the lightweight boxing championship title was:

   a. **Joe Gans**
   b. **Sidney Barthwell**
   c. **Tiger Flowers**
   d. **Mack Iver**

4. The lightweight fighter who was known for his outstanding endurance is:

   a. **Peter Jackson**
   b. **Norvell Lee**
   c. **John Dungee**
   d. **Joe Gans**

5. Who was the first black heavyweight boxing champion of America?

   a. **Garrison Lewis**
   b. **Frank Thompson**
   c. **Peter Jackson**
   d. **George Godfrey**

6. Who was the *first* boxer to ever regain the heavyweight championship?

   a. **Joe Louis**
   b. **Floyd Patterson**
   c. **Muhammad Ali**
   d. **Jack Johnson**

7. The only boxer to hold three titles at the same time was:

   a. Sugar Ray Robinson **c. Henry Armstrong**
   b. Floyd Patterson **d. Joe Walcott**

8. When was Jersey Joe Walcott heavyweight boxing champion?

   a. 1951–52 **c. 1954–55**
   b. 1945–46 **d. 1960–61**

9. In 1932, which one of the following won the featherweight championship?

   a. Dick Tiger **c. Kid Gavilan**
   b. Kid Chocolate **d. Joe Gans**

10. Which one of the following regained the heavyweight boxing crown more times than the others listed?

   a. Joe Louis **c. Sugar Ray Robinson**
   b. Floyd Patterson **d. Jack Johnson**

---

1. Bill Richmond, of Staten Island, N.Y., in the early 1800s 2. Sugar Ray Robinson 3. Joe Gans, on May 12, 1902 4. Joe Gans. He held the lightweight title from 1901 to 1908. However he fought anyone at any weight. He fought three men in one day on July 15, 1901 5. George Godfrey. He weighed only 170 pounds but defeated all who had nerve enough to enter the ring with him. He was matched with John L. Sullivan, but Sullivan simply would not fight a black man 6. Floyd Patterson, when he knocked out Ingemar Johansson in the fifth round on June 20, 1960 7. "Hammerin' " Henry Armstrong, featherweight, 126 pounds; lightweight, 135 pounds; welterweight, 147 pounds 8. 1951–52 9. Kid Chocolate 10. Floyd Patterson

---

BOXING QUIZ 2

Match the following with the correct paragraph. There are twelve possible answers but only ten paragraphs. Some answers may be used more than once.

Jack Johnson	**Tom Molineaux**
Joe Louis	**Joe Frazier**
Joe Gans	**Andy Bowen**
George Dixon	**Kid Chocolate**
Floyd Patterson	**James J. Braddock**
Muhammad Ali	**Sugar Ray Robinson**

1. When he gave up the title in 1949 and announced his retirement, he had an astonishing record: sixty-two fights, fifty-two knock-out victories, nine triumphs by decision and one defeat.

2. On June 22, 1937, Joe Louis defeated him for the heavyweight championship of the world.

3. Known as "Little Chocolate," he was the first black fighter to become a recognized world boxing champion. On March 31, 1891, in Troy, New York, in a bruising battle that went twenty-one rounds, he floored the white title holder, Cal McCarthy, for the featherweight title.

4. He was the first great black heavyweight boxer in the nineteenth century. He fought all the great heavyweights of his day in England and on the Continent. Born a slave in 1784, he is reputed to have gained his freedom with his fists. His greatest fight was against Tom Gribb in 1808 in London. After forty rounds, Gribb won under suspicious circumstances.

5. He was the first black to win the world heavyweight title. He won the title from Burns in 1908 and held it longer than any heavyweight up to the time he lost to Jess Willard in a controversial finish in Cuba in 1915. His life is the topic of the play and movie *The Great White Hope.* His fight weight was 195. He was a shade over six feet tall.

6. He was the first black to hold a boxing title for more than ten years.

7. He was denied a chance for the lightweight title and went on to fight the longest fight in the recorded history of fighting, a 110-round bout with Jack Burke that lasted seven hours and nineteen minutes. It ended in a draw (April 6, 1893).

8. After gaining one victory over Muhammad Ali and losing to him in a later bout, he was defeated for the second straight time by George Foreman.

9. Floyd Patterson, Joe Frazier and George Foreman were former black Olympic boxing champions who went on to become world heavyweight champions. Missing from this group is:

10. He was stripped of his heavyweight title when he refused to be inducted into the U.S. Army.

---

1. Joe Louis 2. James J. Braddock 3. George Dixon 4. Tom Molineaux 5. Jack Johnson 6. Joe Louis was heavyweight champion of the world for nearly twelve years (June 22, 1937, till March 1, 1949) 7. Andy Bowen 8. Joe Frazier 9. Muhammad Ali 10. Muhammad Ali

---

FOOTBALL QUIZ 1

1. This college is known for the number of its alumni in professional football. It has sent dozens of black football stars to the professional ranks beginning with Tank Younger's signing with the Los Angeles Rams in 1946. After Younger's success, professional scouts from all over the country descended on the Louisiana campus to recruit the protégés of Coach Eddie Robinson.

   a. Baton Rouge University
   b. Southern University
   c. Grambling College
   d. Dillard University

2. He was the first nationally known black to play college football. He became a legend at Brown University by continuously contributing to the defeat of Yale and Harvard.

   a. Fritz Pollard | **c. Andrew Brimmer**
   b. Ralph Boston | **d. Earl Graves**

3. He was the first black to play big league professional football. He played with the Akron Indians before they became part of the National Football League.

   a. John Shelton | **c. Fritz Pollard**
   b. Otis Miller | **d. Otis Franklin**

4. In 1974, he was heralded as one of the most successful quarterbacks in the National Football League. He played for the Los Angeles Rams.

   a. Jimmy Harris | **c. J. J. Mayes**
   b. J. J. Plesant | **d. Lester Coleman**

5. The 1974 Heisman Trophy went to him for his outstanding ability as a running back at Ohio State University.

a. Archie Griffin **c. Archie Gresham**
b. Archie Moore **d. Archie Slade**

6. The first black football player elected to the Football Hall of Fame from Rutgers University was:

a. Paul Robeson **c. Jim Blake**
b. Fred "Duke" Slater **d. Roscoe Littlejohn**

7. The first black to score a touchdown in a Rose Bowl game was:

a. Buddy Young **c. Jim Brown**
b. Lenny Ford **d. Daniel Neusom**

8. The first black college football game was played between:

a. Johnson C. Smith University and Lane College
b. Howard University and Morgan State University
c. Johnson C. Smith University and Livingston College
d. Livingston College and Kentucky State College

9. Who was generally thought to be the first black professional football player?

a. Roosevelt Brown **c. Marlin Brisco**
b. Victor Claytor **d. Henry McDonald**

10. The first black football player to be elected to the game's Hall of Fame was:

a. Willard Motley **c. James Gresham**
b. L. Brown Jackson **d. Marion Motley**

1. *Grambling College* 2. *Fritz Pollard* 3. *Fritz Pollard* 4. *Jimmy Harris* 5. *Archie Griffin* 6. *Fred "Duke" Slater* 7. *Buddy Young, of the University of Illinois, on New Year's Day, 1947* 8. *Johnson C. Smith University of Charlotte, N.C., and Livingston College of Salisbury, N.C., on Thanksgiving Day, 1892. Johnson C. Smith (then known as Biddle College) won* 9. *Henry McDonald, who played with the Oxford Pros in 1911. He switched to the Rochester Jeffersons in 1912* 10. *Marion Motley, the indestructible fullback of the Cleveland Browns, in 1968*

FOOTBALL QUIZ 2

1. Who was the black football player who broke the rushing record of the fabled Red Grange of Illinois?

   a. **Jim Brown** c. **J. C. Caroline**
   b. **Roosevelt Brown** d. **Ollie Matson**

2. Sports writers generally agree that the best black football player ever to set foot on a football field is:

   a. **J. C. Caroline** c. **Ollie Matson**
   b. **Jim Brown** d. **Roosevelt Brown**

3. The first black to play football with Cornell University was:

   a. **Bernie Jefferson** c. **Wilmeth Singh**
   b. **Bob Mann** d. **Jerome Holland**

4. The first black football captain at Yale University was:

   a. **Wardell Lott** c. **Reginald Kilgore**
   b. **Levi Jackson** d. **Bill Williams**

5. The first black All-American football player was:

   a. **Jonathan Rogers**
   b. **William Henry Lewis**
   c. **Wesley Brown**
   d. **Andrew Moore**

6. The first black football star to play in the Rose Bowl was:

   a. **Willard Motley**
   b. **L. Brown Jackson**
   c. **Fritz Pollard**
   d. **James Gresham**

7. The first black to play football on a southern college gridiron was:

   a. **Chester Pierce**
   b. **Charles Drew**
   c. **Bud Terrance**
   d. **Ralph Bunche**

8. He is the holder of the all-time ball carrying record in the National Football League. He carried the ball for 12,312 yards and scored 126 touchdowns. He retired from ball playing in 1965 to become a movie star.

   a. **J. J. Walker**
   b. **Jim Brown**
   c. **Fred Williamson**
   d. **Dee Dee Williams**

9. He was considered to be the most successful coach of black college football. As head coach of Florida A & M University, his Rattlers consistently won national championships. Several of his former players are now playing in the American and National conferences of the National Football League. He was elected to the Helms Foundation Hall of Fame in 1961. He retired in 1973.

   a. **Alonzo Gaither**
   b. **"Big House" Gaines**
   c. **Leroy Dues**
   d. **Frank Pellem**

10. He is generally regarded as the greatest running back in the history of college football. He rushed for 1,709 yards in ten games as a senior at the University of Southern California. He scored twenty-two touchdowns in 1968 and was a landslide choice for the Heisman Trophy.

    a. **Elvin Hayes** c. **Matt Woods**
    b. **Floyd McKelpin** d. **O. J. Simpson**

---

1. J. C. Caroline 2. Jim Brown 3. Jerome Holland. He also became president of Hampton Institute and Delaware State College and U.S. ambassador to Sweden 4. Levi Jackson, in 1949 5. William Henry Lewis, who played for Amherst College and Harvard University 6. Fritz Pollard of Brown University in 1916 7. Chester Pierce, of Harvard, played against the University of Virginia at Charlottesville in 1947 8. Jim Brown 9. Alonzo Gaither 10. O. J. Simpson

---

GOLF

1. Who was the greatest black golfer to emerge in the late 1960s?

    a. **Arthur Ashe**
    b. **Lee Elder**
    c. **Gene Ammonds**
    d. **Harold Caison**

2. Who is generally thought to be the first golf club professional in the U.S. born in this country?

    a. **John Shippen**
    b. **John Jenkins**
    c. **John Harris**
    d. **John Maben**

3. When was the first black professional golfers' association founded?

   a. **during the 1930s**
   b. **during the 1940s**
   c. **during the 1950s**
   d. **during the 1920s**

4. Who was the first black golfer to win a "big time" open?

   a. **Lee Elder**
   b. **Charlie Sifford**
   c. **Dan Brooks**
   d. **Alex Grimes**

5. Who was the first black to ever win a major public links tournament?

   a. **Bill Jones, from Birmingham**
   b. **Bill Burroughs, from Dayton**
   c. **Bill Wright, from Kansas City**
   d. **Bill Davis, from Washington, D.C.**

6. Who won the 1974 "title" of "long ball hitter"?

   a. **Lee Elder**
   b. **Jim Dent**
   c. **Roy Graham**
   d. **Charles Jordan**

7. Who was the first black golfer to play in the Masters Tournament in Augusta, Georgia?

   a. **Lee Elder**
   b. **Ernie Pitt**
   c. **Bill Wright**
   d. **Dalk Taylor**

8. Who were the first black golfers signed by golfing equipment manufacturers to endorse their products?

   a. **Charlie Sifford and Ted Rhodes**
   b. **Lee Elder and Zeke Hartsfield**
   c. **Ted Rhodes and Harry Jackson**
   d. **Howard Wheeler and Solomon Hughes**

9. Who was the first black golfer to win the Professional Golfers' Association Tournament?

   a. **Lee Elder**
   b. **Charlie Sifford**
   c. **Bill Wright**
   d. **John Shippen**

10. He was the first black golfer to have an opportunity to qualify for play in the Masters Tournament by virtue of winning a major golf tournament.

   a. **Lee Elder**
   b. **Herb Atkins**
   c. **Frank Westbrook**
   d. **Gene Mulberry**

---

1. Lee Elder 2. John Shippen. The other early pros were imported from Scotland and England. Around 1900, Shippen and his brother Cyrus instructed on some of the exclusive courses in the nation (mostly in the East) 3. during the 1920s. Blacks were not permitted to compete with whites and held their first national tournament in 1926 4. Charlie Sifford at Long Beach, California, in 1957, when he defeated Eric Monti in a sudden-death playoff 5. Bill Wright, from Kansas City, Missouri, a student at Western Washington College, won the National Public Links Golf Championship — the Standish Cup — in 1959 6. Jim Dent 7. Lee Elder 8. Charlie Sifford and Ted Rhodes 9. Charlie Sifford 10. Lee Elder.

HORSE RACING

1. During what period in history did blacks dominate the sport of kings (horse racing)?

   a. **immediately following the Civil War**
   b. **immediately following World War I**
   c. **immediately following the Revolutionary War**
   d. **immediately following the Spanish-American War**

2. The first black jockey to win international fame was:

a. **Willie Simms** c. **Clarence Reed**
b. **Jimmy Winkfield** d. **Oliver Lewis**

3. The first black female jockey was:

a. **Velma Strayhorne** c. **Fannie Pye**
b. **Margaret Jenkins** d. **Cheryl White**

4. The famous black rider who won the Kentucky Derby in 1877 rode a horse named Baden-Baden. The jockey's name was:

a. **Bill Walker** c. **Maurice Alston**
b. **Charles Miller** d. **Oliver Lewis**

5. The finest black rider of the 1870s was:

a. **Bill Walker** c. **Nat Fairfax**
b. **Jess Conley** d. **Ree Payne**

6. The first Kentucky Derby winner was a jockey named:

a. **Jimmy Winkfield** c. **Clarence Reed**
b. **Oliver Lewis** d. **Wardell Lott**

7. The last black jockey to ride in the Kentucky Derby (1911) was:

a. **Bill Johnson** c. **Richard Blanks**
b. **Jess Conley** d. **Willie Gardner**

8. The first black jockey to be elected to the racing Hall of Fame (1902) was:

a. **Jimmy Winkfield** c. **Clarence Reed**
b. **Isaac Murphy** d. **Dudley McDonald**

9. The black jockey who established records in the Kentucky Derby that have never been equaled is:

   a. **Isaac Murphy** c. **Larry Williams**
   b. **Jeremiah Parson** d. **Norris Coleman**

10. The first jockey to ride three Kentucky Derby winners was:

   a. **Isaac Murphy** c. **Tedd Carr**
   b. **Al Barringer** d. **William Oliver**

---

1. immediately following the Civil War 2. Willie Simms 3. Cheryl White. She rode for the first time on June 15, 1971, and won for the first time on September 2, 1971 4. Bill Walker 5. Bill Walker 6. Oliver Lewis, who rode a horse named Aristedes in 1875 7. Jess Conley 8. Isaac Murphy 9. Isaac Murphy 10. Isaac Murphy. He rode Buchanan in 1884, Riley in 1890 and Kingman in 1891

TRACK AND FIELD

1. In what year and city did blacks enter Olympic games competition?

   a. **1908 in London** c. **1924 in Paris**
   b. **1904 in St. Louis** d. **1936 in Berlin**

2. Who was the first black to win an Olympic gold medal?

   a. **De Hart Hubbard** c. **Jesse Owens**
   b. **Rafer Johnson** d. **Edward Gourdin**

3. What are the names of the two black Olympic champions who, in Mexico City in 1968, gave the raised black-gloved fist salute during the playing of "The Star Spangled Banner"?

   a. **Ron Freeman and Lee Evans**
   b. **Larry James and Ron Freeman**
   c. **John Carlos and Tommy Smith**
   d. **Stan Wright and Larry James**

4. Who was the first black athlete to win a medal in the Olympic games?

   a. **George Poage**
   b. **Melvin Chapman**
   c. **Lorenzo Wright**
   d. **Leroy Dues**

5. Who was the first person to broad jump more than twenty-five feet?

   a. **Jesse Owens**
   b. **Rafer Johnson**
   c. **Edward Gourdin**
   d. **Mat Whitlock**

6. At Mexico City in 1968, the U.S. won fifteen gold medals in track and field. How many were won by black Americans?

   a. **6**
   b. **0**
   c. **10**
   d. **13**

7. Who is generally considered to be the greatest national track hero ever produced in the United States?

   a. **Jesse Owens**
   b. **Rafer Johnson**
   c. **John Carlos**
   d. **Tommy Wright**

8. Who was the track great who, in seventy-four minutes at the University of Michigan on May 25, 1934, broke three world records and tied a fourth?

   a. Lou Hudson **c. Stanley Mullins**
   b. Harvey Melton **d. Jesse Owens**

9. Who was the first black to hold the title of "the world's fastest human"? In 1914 at the University of Southern California, he eclipsed the world 100-yard-dash record with a spectacular 9.6 seconds.

   a. Bob Hayes **c. Howard Drew**
   b. John Carlos **d. Po Taylor**

10. Who of the following is regarded as the fastest female sprinter of all time? She also won three gold medals in the 1960 Olympics.

   a. Wilma Rudolph **c. Althea Gibson**
   b. Ora Washington **d. Deborah Price**

---

1. 1904 in St. Louis 2. De Hart Hubbard, of the University of Michigan, in Paris in 1924. The event was the broad jump 3. John Carlos and Tommy Smith 4. George Poage, an outstanding hurdler and quarter-miler, in 1904 in St. Louis, Missouri 5. Edward Gourdin, in the 1920s 6. 10 7. Jesse Owens 8. Jesse Owens 9. Howard Drew 10. Wilma Rudolph

---

TENNIS

1. One of the most spectacular black women tennis players of all times was:

   a. Darlene Hartman **c. Cynthia Thomas**
   b. Joyce White **d. Althea Gibson**

2. The first black to compete in the United States Lawn Tennis Association championship competition was:

   a. **Althea Gibson, from Harlem, in August, 1950**
   b. **Darlene Hooks, from High Point, North Carolina, in 1950**
   c. **Cora Robinson, from Little Rock, Arkansas, in 1951**
   d. **Vera M. King, from Mobile, Alabama, in 1951**

3. The first winner of the new U.S. Open Championship at Forest Hills Stadium in New York (September 9, 1968) was:

   a. **Willie Snuggs**
   b. **Arthur Ashe**
   c. **Rickey Harris**
   d. **Milford Vaughn**

4. The first black man ever to be a finalist at Wimbledon was:

   a. **Talley Holmes**
   b. **Norman Coleman**
   c. **Ronald Williams**
   d. **Arthur Ashe**

5. The first black tennis player to become the U.S. men's amateur tennis champion (1968) was:

   a. **Talley Holmes**
   b. **Delbert Russell**
   c. **Richard Hemphill**
   d. **Arthur Ashe**

6. The greatest black female tennis player who ever lived is generally thought to be:

   a. **Ora Washington**
   b. **Winifred King**
   c. **Katie Fillmore**
   d. **Elizabeth Woods**

7. The first black tennis tournament was organized in 1898 by a minister named:

   a. **J. L. Lightfoot**
   b. **W. W. Walker**
   c. **Bishop H. L. Grace**
   d. **Rev. John Shippen**

8. The first black international tennis tournament was held on September 21, 1974, in the city of:

   a. **Silver Spring, Maryland**
   b. **Atlantic City, New Jersey**
   c. **Washington, D.C.**
   d. **Grosse Pointe, Michigan**

9. The first black tennis player to join the U.S. Davis Cup tennis team was:

   a. **Arthur Ashe**
   b. **Rick Hemphill**
   c. **Howard Cameron**
   d. **Harry McDavid**

10. The first black woman to win the Wimbledon tennis championship was:

   a. **Florence Smith**
   b. **Aretha Johnson**
   c. **Althea Gibson**
   d. **Delores Willis**

---

1. Althea Gibson 2. Althea Gibson, from Harlem, in August, 1950 3. Arthur Ashe 4. Arthur Ashe 5. Arthur Ashe 6. Ora Washington. She was undefeated for twelve years in a row. She began her tennis career in 1924 7. W. W. Walker 8. Washington, D.C. 9. Arthur Ashe 10. Althea Gibson

---

MISCELLANEOUS SPORTS

1. When and where was the first black-owned bowling league organized?

   a. **in 1941 in Cleveland, Ohio**
   b. **in 1942 in Philadelphia, Pennsylvania**
   c. **in 1940 in New York, New York**
   d. **in 1943 in Detroit, Michigan**

2. What black was known as the fastest bicycle racer in the world?

   a. **Ralph Ellison of Pittsburgh, Pennsylvania**
   b. **Donald Martin of Greensboro, North Carolina**
   c. **Wright Filmore of New York, New York**
   d. **Marshall W. Taylor of Indianapolis, Indiana**

3. The most outstanding black auto racer (though he never drove in the Indianapolis 500) was:

   a. **Rojo Jack**
   b. **Joe Trigg**
   c. **David Blake**
   d. **Calvin Fields**

4. The first black to compete in organized ice hockey was:

   a. **Alonzo Smith of the Washington Beavers**
   b. **Reginald Harvey of the Philadelphia Magpies**
   c. **Andrew Bryant of the Detroit Redwings**
   d. **Art Dorrington of the Johnstown Jets**

5. The first black to compete in the Pikes Peak Hill Climb auto race was:

   a. **Harold Caison**
   b. **Elbert J. Grayson**
   c. **Berton Groves**
   d. **Alfred O. Taylor**

6. Who was the black man that was the very first director of physical education at Harvard University?

   a. **L. Brown Jackson**
   b. **Walter Ford**
   c. **Abram M. Hewlett**
   d. **Stanley Wainwright**

7. The first black to race in a varsity crew was:

   a. **Thomas B. Stanford**
   b. **Emmett Long**
   c. **Ted Lawrence**
   d. **Joe Trigg**

8. The first black to compete in organized swimming was:

   a. **Wendell Cox** c. **Samuel E. Barnes**
   b. **Clarence Catliff** d. **George P. Wheeler**

9. The first black American to achieve distinction in fencing was:

   a. **Ernest Baxter at Rutgers University in 1938**
   b. **William S. King at Howard University in 1940**
   c. **Isaac Floyd at Bradley University in 1941**
   d. **Reginald Howard at Federal City College in 1968**

10. Who was the great athlete who excelled in virtually every sport at Amherst College (track, basketball, football, and baseball) and went on to become a world-famous physician/surgeon/medical researcher?

   a. **Charles R. Drew** c. **Jackson C. Davis**
   b. **Rudolph J. Snowden** d. **York C. Campbell**

---

1. in 1941 in Cleveland, Ohio 2. Marshall W. Taylor of Indianapolis, Indiana. He was the hero of millions here and overseas during the 1890s. He won the American sprint championship three years in a row and defeated the best cyclists in Europe and Australia 3. Rojo Jack 4. Art Dorrington of the Johnstown Jets 5. Berton Groves 6. Abram M. Hewlett 7. Joe Trigg of Syracuse University 8. Clarence Catliff. He captained Detroit's Cass Technical High's team in 1925 9. Ernest Baxter at Rutgers University in 1938 10. Charles R. Drew

---

Supreme Court and the Law

The men sitting on the Supreme Court in this country have made decisions both favorable and unfavorable to blacks. However, this section does not deal primarily with the negative decisions; rather, it focuses on those that have been positive and necessary for liberation from oppression.

In recent times, the Court has written favorable decisions in the areas of housing, public accommodations, civil rights and education. It may be that most of these landmark decisions fit well into the civil rights category, but often the language in the legal documents does not include the term "civil rights."

It was the Supreme Court that struck down the laws restricting black participation in the political process. While *Brown* v. *Board of Education of Topeka, Kansas* is considered a landmark case of national importance, the court was busy reviewing other cases germane to the civil rights movement. The foundation for a positive decision in this case was laid several years before its appearance in the courts. The Court that Earl Warren convened sought, as one of its tasks, to help blacks achieve full citizenship in these United States of America.

SUPREME COURT AND THE LAW QUIZ 1

1. When did the U.S. Supreme Court order school integration "with all deliberate speed"?

   a. **May 31, 1954**
   b. **May 31, 1955**
   c. **May 31, 1956**
   d. **May 31, 1957**

2. When did the U.S. Supreme Court rule that busing is a constitutionally acceptable method of destroying the dual school systems?

   a. **April 20, 1970**
   b. **April 20, 1971**
   c. **April 20, 1972**
   d. **April 20, 1973**

3. When was the "separate but equal" doctrine handed down?

   a. **in 1863**
   b. **in 1869**
   c. **in 1876**
   d. **in 1879**

4. The first black to be accredited as a Supreme Court lawyer was:

   a. **Harold Floyd**
   b. **Eugene Hall**
   c. **Emmitt Long**
   d. **John Rock**

5. What were the Civil War amendments to the Constitution?

   a. **the Eleventh and Thirteenth amendments**
   b. **the Eleventh and Fifteenth amendments**
   c. **the Thirteenth and Fifteenth amendments**
   d. **all of the above**

6. In 1865, Congress ratified a constitutional amendment and established the Freedmen's Bureau. The amendment was the:

   a. **Eleventh**
   b. **Thirteenth**
   c. **Fifteenth**
   d. **Seventeenth**

7. When and in what case did the U.S. Supreme Court enter the field of employment discrimination in the twentieth century?

   a. **in 1944, in the case of *Randolph* v. *the B&O Railroad***
   b. **in 1944, in the case of *Steele* v. *Louisville and Nashville Railroad***
   c. **in 1940, in the case of *Brown* v. *Macy's Department Store***
   d. **in 1940, in the case of *Guest* v. *Gimbel's Department Store***

8. On July 28, 1869, an amendment to the Constitution was ratified, establishing "equal protection" for all citizens under the laws of the U.S. Constitution. It was the:

   a. **Eleventh Amendment**
   b. **Twelfth Amendment**
   c. **Thirteenth Amendment**
   d. **Fourteenth Amendment**

9. Which one of the following Supreme Court cases involved public accommodations?

   a. *Katzenbach* v. *McClung* (1964)
   b. *Holmes* v. *Atlanta* (1955)
   c. *Gayle* v. *Browder* (1956)
   d. *Rice* v. *Arnold* (1950)

10. Which one of the following Supreme Court cases involved education?

   a. *Moore* v. *Dempsey* (1923)
   b. *Sweatt* v. *Painter* (1950)
   c. *Lee* v. *Mississippi* (1948)
   d. *Hollins* v. *Oklahoma* (1935)

---

*1. May 31, 1955 2. April 20, 1971 3. in 1869 (*Plessy *v.* Ferguson*) 4. John S. Rock, a teacher, dentist, physician and a lawyer, born in Salem, New Jersey, in 1825 5. all of the above. The Eleventh Amendment (1868) conferred national and state citizenship on "all persons born or naturalized in the U.S." The Thirteenth Amendment (1865) abolished slavery everywhere. The Emancipation Proclamation (1863) had only abolished slavery in the states engaged in rebellion. The Fifteenth Amendment (1870) gave blacks the right to vote 6. Thirteenth 7. in 1944, in the case of* Steele *v.* Louisville and Nashville Railroad *8. Fourteenth Amendment* 9. Katzenbach *v.* McClung *(1964)* *10.* Sweatt *v.* Painter *(1950)*

SUPREME COURT AND THE LAW QUIZ 2

Match the following with the correct paragraph. There are twelve possible answers but only ten paragraphs. Some answers may be used more than once.

Lee* v. *Mississippi	***Bond* v. *Floyd***
Thurgood Marshall	***Sweatt* v. *Painter***
Rice* v. *Arnold	**Jonathan J. Wright**
Katzenbach* v. *McClung	**Benjamin Roberts**
Dred Scott	**Nat Turner**
Brown* v. *Board of Education	***Moore* v. *Dempsey***

1. He was the most famous slave of his time. In "free" territory he brought suit for his freedom. The Supreme Court ruled against him and thereby denied blacks the right of citizenship. He was later freed by his owner.

2. Born in 1908, he was a civil rights lawyer, a U.S. circuit judge, was appointed solicitor general of the U.S., and on June 13, 1967, became an associate justice of the Supreme Court.

3. He filed the first school integration suit on behalf of his daughter in Boston, in November, 1849. The Massachusetts Supreme Court rejected the suit and established a "separate but equal" precedent.

4. He was the first black state Supreme Court justice elected to a full term in South Carolina.

5. This case (January 19, 1948) involved a seventeen-year-old black who was convicted of assault with the intent to rape, his conviction having been based on a confession which had been allegedly coerced.

6. This case involved the successful attempt to abolish segregation on a Miami, Florida, golf course that was owned and operated by the city.

7. This was the first of two critical admissions cases. Decided in 1966, it established the right of a legally qualified elected official to serve in his state legislature despite political statements unpopular with that legislature.

8. This case (May 17, 1954) involved the practice of denying black children equal access to state public schools due to state laws requiring or permitting racial segregation.

9. The black petitioner in this case (June 5, 1950) was refused admission to the law school of the University of Texas on the grounds that equivalent facilities were available in another Texas school open only to blacks.

10. It was a "due process" case (February 19, 1923) that resulted from an outgrowth of an Arkansas race riot. One white man was killed and several persons were injured. Twelve blacks were sentenced to death and sixty-seven to lengthy prison terms.

---

1. Dred Scott 2. Thurgood Marshall 3. Benjamin Roberts 4. Jonathan J. Wright **5. Lee v. Mississippi 6. Rice v. Arnold 7. Bond v. Floyd 8. Brown v. Board of Education 9. Sweatt v. Painter 10. Moore v. Dempsey**

Suggested Reading List

Adams, Russell L. *Great Negroes Past and Present.* Chicago: Afro-American Press, 1964.

Anderson, Jervis. *A. Philip Randolph: A Biographical Portrait.* New York: Harcourt Brace Jovanovich, Inc., 1973.

Baker, Houston A. *Black Literature in America.* New York: McGraw-Hill Book Company, 1971.

Bennett, Lerone, Jr. *Pioneers in Protest.* Baltimore: Penguin Books, Inc., 1968.

Bennett, Lerone, Jr. *Before the Mayflower: A History of Black America.* Chicago: Johnson Publishing Co., Inc., 1969.

Bergman, Peter M. and Mort N. Bergman. *The Chronological History of the Negro in America.* New York: The New American Library, Inc., 1969.

Blassingame, John W. *The Slave Community.* New York: Oxford University Press, 1972.

Bontemps, Arna W. *Famous Negro Athletes.* New York: Dodd, Mead & Company, 1964.

Bullock, Henry A. *A History of Negro Education in the South.* New York: Praeger Publishers, 1970.

Carmichael, Stokely and Charles V. Hamilton. *Black Power:*

The Politics of Liberation in America. New York: Random House, 1967.

Carnegie Corporation, *The Higher Education of Blacks in the United States.* New York: 1973.

Cogan, Lee. *Negroes for Medicine.* Baltimore: Johns-Hopkins Press, 1968.

Curry, Richard O. (ed). *The Abolitionists, Reformers or Fanatics.* New York: Holt, Rinehart & Winston, 1965.

Dann, Martin E. (ed). *The Black Press 1827–1890.* New York: G. P. Putnam's Sons, 1971.

Detweiler, Frederick G. *The Negro Press in the United States.* College Park, Maryland: McGrath Publishing Company, 1968.

Edmonds, Helen G. *Black Faces in High Places.* New York: Harcourt Brace Jovanovich, Inc., 1971.

Edwards, Harry. *The Revolt of the Black Athlete.* New York: The Free Press, 1969.

Fisher, Paul L. and Ralph L. Lowenstein. *Race and the News Media.* New York: Praeger Publishers, 1968.

Franklin, John Hope. *From Slavery to Freedom.* New York: Alfred A. Knopf, 1965.

Frazier, E. Franklin. *The Negro Church in America.* New York: Schocken Books, 1964.

Ginsberg, Eli (ed). *Business Leadership and the Negro Crisis.* New York: McGraw-Hill, 1968.

Greene, Robert E. *Black Defenders of America: 1775–1973.* Chicago: Johnson Publishing Company, Inc., 1974.

Grier, William H., and Price M. Cobbs. *Black Rage.* New York: Basic Books, 1968.

Hatch, James V. *Black Image on the American Stage.* New York: DBS Publications, Inc., 1970.

Jacobson, Julius. *The Negro and the American Labor Movement.* New York: Doubleday & Company, Inc., 1968.

Knowles, Louis L. and Kenneth Prewitt (eds.). *Institutional Racism in America.* Englewood Cliffs: Prentice-Hall, Inc., 1969.

Lee, Irvin H. *Negro Medal of Honor Men.* New York: Dodd, Mead & Company, 1967.

Lindenmeyer, Otto. *Black History: Lost, Stolen or Strayed.* New York: Avon Books, 1970.

Logan, Rayford W., and Irvin S. Cohen. *The American Negro: Old World Background and New World Experience.* Boston: Houghton Mifflin Company, 1970.

Lyndon, Michael. *Boogie Lightning.* New York: The Dial Press, 1974.

MacDonald, Stephen (ed). *Business and Blacks.* Princeton: Dow Jones Books, 1970.

Marshall, Ray. *The Negro Worker.* New York: Random House, 1967.

Middleton, Richard. *Pop Music and the Blues.* London: Victor Gallancz Ltd., 1972.

Miller, Loren. *The Petitioners: The Story of the Supreme Court of the U.S. and the Negro.* New York: Pantheon Books, 1966.

Orr, Jack. *The Black Athlete.* New York: The Lion Press, 1969.

Penn, I. Garland. *The Afro-American Press and Its Editors.* New York: Arno Press and *The New York Times,* 1969.

Ploski, Harry A. and Ernest Kaiser. *The Negro Almanac.* New York: The Bellwether Company, 1971.

Powers, Anne (ed). *Blacks in American Movies.* Metuchen, New Jersey: The Scarecrow Press, Inc., 1974.

Quarles, Benjamin. *Allies for Freedom: Blacks and John Brown.* New York: Oxford University Press, 1974.

Reimers, David. *The Black Man in America.* (Since Reconstruction). New York: Thomas Y. Crowell Company, 1970.

Saunders, Doris E. (ed). *The Ebony Handbook.* Chicago: Johnson Publishing Company, Inc., 1974.

Seham, Max, M.D. *Blacks and American Medical Care.* Minneapolis: The University of Minnesota Press, 1973.

Southern, Eileen (ed). *Readings in Black Music.* New York: W. W. Norton & Company, Inc., 1971.

Sullivan, Leon H. *Build Brother Build.* Philadelphia: Macrae Smith Company, 1969.

Turner, Darwin T. (ed). *Afro-American Writers.* New York: Appleton-Century-Crofts, Educational Division, 1970.

Tussman, Joseph (ed). *U.S. Supreme Court.* (The Supreme Court on Racial Discrimination) New York: Oxford University Press, 1963.

Wagner, Jean. *Black Poets of the United States: From Paul Laurence Dunbar to Langston Hughes.* Urbana: The University of Illinois Press, 1973.

Walton, Hanes, Jr. *Black Politics.* Philadelphia: J. B. Lippincott Company, 1972.

Washington, Joseph R., Jr. *Black Religion: The Negro and Christianity in the United States.* Boston: Beacon Press, 1964.

Williams, Ethel L. and Clifton L. Brown. *Afro-American Religious Studies.* Metuchen, New Jersey: The Scarecrow Press, 1972.

Woodson, Carter G. *Mis-education of the Negro.* District of Columbia: The Associated Publishers, Inc., 1969.

Young, Andrew S. N. *Negro Firsts in Sports.* Chicago: Johnson Publishing Company, Inc., 1963.

Index

The Authors

Dr. Clarence N. Blake is a Professor of Education at Federal City College of the District of Columbia.

Dr. Donald F. Martin is Assistant Professor of Education and Assistant Director of University Extension, University of North Carolina, Chapel Hill.